NEW DAD'S FIRST YEAR

EASY PROVEN METHODS TO RAISE A HEALTHY,
HAPPY CHILD. INCLUDES MONTH BY MONTH
GUIDE AND PRACTICAL BABY CARE TIPS

NEW DAD SUPPORT

CONTENTS

FREE BONUSES

Free Bonus #1   Baby Financial Planning

In this book, you will learn all about the financial considerations of having a baby.

Free Bonus #2 10 Activities to Learn Parenting Skills

In this book, you will get tips on how to build parenting skills even before the baby is born.

Free Bonus #3 Authentic Connections

In this book, you will learn new skills to help you nurture your connection with your partner and bring it to a whole new level.

INTRODUCTION

Remember the day you found out there was a baby on the way? Hard to believe that was less than a year ago. And now, after nine whole months of your partner's pregnancy, the moment has come. You have arrived: a new dad.

Wouldn't it be nice if it were that simple? The reality is, the journey is really just getting started. That might sound intimidating - and it is! But it's only intimidating (and a little scary) because it's the first step in learning more about yourself, your partner, and your little guy or gal than you ever imagined possible. And as you'll find out this year, the first steps always come with some trepidation.

Back in the day, dads were distant figures sort of looming in the background. They tended to be less involved - if not entirely uninvolved - in the birthing process, and often they weren't actively involved in their children's lives. Thankfully, the tide is turning. If you're reading this book, you are part of that change.

More and more research shows that dads who are involved in their child's life have a tremendous impact on their baby's growth, development, and, most importantly - happiness. And what's really amazing is that the flip side also holds true. Being an active participant in your baby's first year is immeasurably fulfilling. There are sleepless nights and challenges, sure - but it's beyond worth it.

But what about those sleepless nights and challenges? That's what this book aims to help you navigate. You'll notice each chapter is divided into eight sections. Here's a little background as to why I chose each category, and what you can expect to learn in each.

Milestones

Ah, milestones. I have a love/hate relationship with them. I love them because they're a great way to gauge whether your baby is on track. Let's be honest: every parent, at some point or another, asks this question: "Is my baby *normal*?" And by that, we usually mean: Is he or she doing everything she is *supposed* to do at this age/ stage of development?" This is where milestones are really convenient.

But this is also where the hate part comes in. Because although it's not a bad thing to have standards, the fact is, every baby is different. I know that's kind of a cliche, but as a dad of six, I mean it from the bottom of my heart. Every baby is *truly* different, and milestones should never be taken as dogmatic truths about your baby's development.

If you become concerned about your baby not reaching his or her milestones, be sure to discuss this with your pediatrician. While it's normal for there to be variations in milestone timetables, sometimes dramatic differences might indicate an underlying problem, and often the sooner your doctor can intervene, the better.

Feeding

Eating seems like a pretty basic thing, and it is - but it's also the most important thing your baby will learn to do this year. And just because something is natural doesn't mean it's easy!

If your partner has decided to breastfeed, there will be a lot to learn in the first few months, especially, and she will need your support. I've included all my best advice for supporting her in her decision to breastfeed in the following pages.

Not all families decide that breastfeeding is for them, though, and that's okay! There are so many healthy formula alternatives out there to choose from if that is what's best for your family's needs. In this book, you will find advice for bottle feeding your baby, introducing solid food, and when it's time, gradually weaning your baby off the bottle. So we'll cover all the bases, regardless of your family's feeding choices.

Sleeping

If you've heard you'll spend the first year of your baby's life as a sleep-deprived dad, rest assured this is only partially true. There are peaks and valleys, and in this book, I've tried to prepare you for some of the sleep challenges your baby (and you and your partner) might face this year.

You'll also find advice for safe sleep, sleep schedules, and sleep training. Because let's face it: while eating might be the most important thing your baby does this year, sleeping is probably at the top of the list for you and your partner.

Bonding With Baby

When I first became a dad, I heard a doctor say something that has really stuck with me: "A baby's wants are a baby's needs." This goes for eating, sleeping, and bonding.

Bonding is often thought of as an "extra" need for babies, but nothing could be further from the truth. Physical touch, communication, cuddling - all these things are good for your baby's development as well as your relationship. It's no surprise, then, that you might notice a lot of overlap between bonding and learning. The deeper your bond with your baby, the more he or she will learn from you.

Learning

Your baby's brain will double in size during the first year of life, and he or she will experience amazing neurological development. All the physical changes your baby will go through - from learning to eat, to crawling, to walking - are dependent on brain development. As noted by the Urban Child Institute, there are three primary areas of the brain that will grow rapidly during year one, and each area is responsible for specific skills :

1. The Cerebellum: Helps with motor skill development and body control.
2. The Visual Cortex: Responsible for interpretation of visual input and recognition
3. The Limbic Structure: Controls memory and emotion

Although brain development is critical during year one,

learning in the first year doesn't require fancy interactive toys or expensive baby gear. In each of the following chapters, you will find simple ways to encourage your baby's neurological development, as well as build fine and gross motor skills.

Keeping Baby Safe

Knowing your home is safe and secure is a key to less stressful parenting. While a lot of these preparations have probably already been made, I've included reminders in each chapter about things to do at each stage of development. You'll also find tips for keeping your baby safe when he or she becomes more mobile - things get really interesting then!

How is Mom?

Your partner's body has gone through enormous changes over the last nine months - and now that your baby is here, the changes don't stop! Supporting your partner in the first year is crucial for her health, recovery, and mental well-being. Each chapter has tips for ways to help her take care of herself, from getting back to exercise, to breastfeeding support, to recognizing the signs of postpartum depression.

How is Dad?

With all the excitement this first year holds, don't forget to take care of yourself. But that's sometimes easier said than done! During crazy times you might not even know what your own needs are because you're so caught up in being a new dad. I've included monthly ideas for taking care of yourself and balancing work, life, and your own self-care.

A final note: this book does not discuss pregnancy, which is really when all this begins. If you haven't read my book on the first nine months of your partner's pregnancy, check it out!

Overall, here's the takeaway I want you to walk away with as you read this book. When you find yourself overwhelmed by all the demands of the parenting "scene" - because I guarantee, you will - **take a step back.** Get off social media and the internet. Close your eyes and think of the moment you held your baby for the first time. That feeling - that's the heart of it.

I hope this book helps you learn how to change diapers, support your partner, and bond with your baby. But more than anything, I hope it helps you hold onto that feeling. Because that's what this dad thing is all about.

CHAPTER 1
BIRTH AND FIRST DAY

WE READ THE BOOKS, took the classes, and did the preparation. As my partner and I walked into our 38-week appointment with our OBGYN, we felt confident and ready for what we were sure would be one of our last appointments before an uncomplicated, natural, vaginal delivery.

There was just one small detail we hadn't anticipated: our baby was breech (head-up instead of the proper head-down position), which meant things would be different from what we expected. After an unsuccessful attempt to turn the baby into a head-down position, my partner went into labor. Within 24 hours of that 38-week appointment, our first baby - a girl - was born.

I was totally enamored with my little girl and amazed at my partner's strength. But I couldn't help but also feel overwhelmed. Years later, my memory of the first 24 hours is a total blur.

Looking back, I realize I felt overwhelmed because even though we prepared for what we thought would happen, **we failed to prepare for the unexpected.**

There are a lot of factors that are totally out of your control when it comes to being a new dad. But one thing that you *can* control is how you prepare and the knowledge you obtain before this crazy, life-changing event happens.

With that in mind, here's what you need to know about birth and the first day after your baby is born.

ROUTINE VAGINAL DELIVERY

What It Is

"Vaginal delivery" is a pretty big blanket term, and the specific type of vaginal delivery will dramatically affect your first 24 hours post-birth.

Generally speaking, a vaginal delivery is considered "routine" if the following criteria are met:

1. Your partner progresses through the normal stages of labor, with or without pain medication
2. Baby is delivered in a head-down position (in medical jargon, this is called "vertex")
3. Baby takes his or her first breath without any medical intervention aside from a nasal aspirator to clear the lungs
4. The final pushing stage progresses smoothly with minimal stalling and no need for intervention (i.e., forceps or cesarean section).

There are definitely situations when c-sections or operative vaginal deliveries are medically necessary, but in most cases, a routine vaginal delivery is the least complicated way to deliver a baby.

It's totally normal for a routine vaginal delivery to take quite a long time - I'm talking like 24 hours or longer. It's definitely an endurance game!

What to Expect After Delivery:

Once your baby is born, your partner will deliver the placenta while the nurses check on baby to make sure all is well and take initial measurements. The placenta is normally "born" within an hour after baby, so if it's taking longer your doctor may administer medicine to speed things along. In the first hour, your baby will also receive newborn tests and any medication you've opted to have administered, such as the vitamin K injection to help with blood clotting and antibiotic eye ointment to prevent eye infections. The doctor will also evaluate your baby's Apgar score (more on that to come).

Then it's time to begin nursing if your partner has chosen to breastfeed. This can be trickier than it sounds! For the first few days, your partner's body produces a substance called colostrum to nourish the baby during the transition into the outside world. Colostrum is packed with all the nutrients the baby needs to adjust. Your partner might feel like she's not providing enough milk, but she is. The baby's stomach is the size of a marble at this point, so it doesn't take much!

Understandably, soreness in the pelvic region is very common in the first 24 hours after vaginal delivery, especially if she experienced any tearing during the process. The hospital should provide pain relief, as well as pads and ice packs to help with that. Your partner might also dread going to the bathroom for the first time - again, understandably! Provide high-fiber snacks to help move things along, and make sure she always has a bottle of water nearby to help her stay hydrated.

NON-ROUTINE VAGINAL DELIVERY

What It Is

A lot of people don't realize that a c-section isn't the only kind of operative delivery. Sometimes interventions need to happen during a routine vaginal birth. These are considered "operative" or "assisted" vaginal deliveries. There are two types:

1. Forceps-assisted delivery: This is when doctors use medical equipment called forceps to help ease baby's head out of the birth canal.
2. Vacuum-assisted delivery: Like forceps delivery, during a vacuum-assisted birth the doctor will use a suction cup to draw baby out of the birth canal during the pushing stage.

According to the ACOG, 3 out of every 100 vaginal deliveries will require one of these interventions. So why might this happen?

The most common reason is that the pushing stage of labor has gone on a really long time, and mom just needs help. Pushing is insanely hard work, and when it comes after 24+ hours of painful labor, assistance is sometimes required. The baby might also be in a difficult position, which can make a vaginal delivery more challenging.

Additionally, your baby might not tolerate labor well and show signs of distress, such as heart rate fluctuations, leading the doctors to decide they need to get baby out, stat! An operative delivery shaves a lot of time off of a routine vaginal delivery timeline, which is often in baby's (and mom's) best interest.

What to Expect After Delivery:

The first 24 hours after an operative vaginal delivery are similar to routine vaginal delivery. Your partner will be very sore and should rest as much as possible. In the long term, healing can take longer due to perineal tearing, which is much more common during operative deliveries.

An operative vaginal delivery might sound intense, but it's generally considered to be less complicated than a c-section. Just be aware that your partner's recovery will be more challenging than it would be for a routine vaginal delivery.

C-SECTION

What It Is

One in three babies in the United States is born via cesarean section or c-section. There are many reasons your baby might need to be delivered via c-section, including failure to progress, fluctuations in heart rate, or fetal positioning. Some conditions your partner may develop during pregnancy might also make a c-section the safest option, such as infections, high blood pressure, and issues with the placenta.

There are two types of c-sections, each of which has its own specific considerations:

1. Emergency c-section: A c-section that takes place as an emergency intervention due to conditions that unfold during the labor process.
2. Scheduled/elective c-section: A c-section that is planned in advance due to conditions that develop during pregnancy. These are typically safer and less complicated than emergency c-sections.

During a c-section, the doctor will administer an epidural and make two incisions: the first through your partner's skin and abdominal wall and the second one into the uterus to deliver the baby. Once the baby is safely delivered, and the placenta has been removed, the doctor will close up the incision site, either with staples, surgical glue, or surgical thread.

What to Expect After Delivery:

The first 24 hours after a c-section are a little different from a vaginal delivery. Your partner will be pretty sore in the abdominal area once the epidural wears off, even with pain medicine. Many women find taking their first steps post-cesarean to be very difficult, so reassure her that this is normal and that she has plenty of time to get back on her feet.

Depending on the reasons for the c-section, there may be more interruptions from nurses post-cesarean. This is just to make sure your partner's vitals are good and that there are no problems with the incision, as well as to do routine checks on baby.

In the first 24 hours, it is totally fine for mom to stay in bed as much as possible, although some hospitals might want her to try to walk one time to prevent blood clots in the legs. Most women stay on pain medication for at least a week after a c-section - it is major abdominal surgery, after all! Encourage your partner to rest as much as possible and not rush things.

IF YOUR BABY WAS BORN PREMATURE

A baby is considered premature if birth occurs before 37 weeks. Since many developmental processes take place during the final three weeks of pregnancy, a premature birth might mean a longer stay in the hospital and a more complicated Day One.

There are three big priorities immediately following a premature birth:

1. **Get Baby Warm:** This is the case for all newborns, but especially for premie babies who can be tiny! They need help thermoregulating and might need to be put on a heating pad or in an incubator to help their body temperature rise.
2. **Establish a Good Breathing Pattern:** The medical team will immediately check baby's heart rate and might need to use suction to help baby clear his or her lungs. Again, this is also common for non-premature babies, especially those with low birth weight, but is more likely if your baby is born early. If baby is struggling to breathe, the medical team might need to use a face mask, breathing tube, or breathing machine to provide some assistance.

What to Expect After Delivery:

Depending on how premature your baby is and the circumstances surrounding his or her birth, a NICU stay may be required. The medical team will evaluate your baby's condition and decide on a case-by-case basis.

Keep in mind that if your baby was born at less than 34 weeks gestation, your partner probably won't be able to breastfeed in the first 24 hours. If breastfeeding is important to her, take this time to discuss strategies to build milk supply with the hospital lactation team.

A cool fact: breastmilk that moms make for premie babies has higher protein content and also contains lipase, which helps the baby digest the milk more easily since the digestive system hasn't had as much time to develop.

For the first year of your baby's life - and probably even for the first two years - he or she will probably hit milestones later than the average full-term baby. This is totally normal and no need for concern. Nevertheless, I know firsthand that parents of premies might feel like their baby is "behind." When our son was born four weeks early, I worried that he would never catch up, but eventually he did! Now, nine years later, you would never know he was only four pounds at birth!

One way to ease your mind is to determine your baby's adjust age, right from the start. To do this, start with your child's actual age, or the number of weeks since birth. Then subtract the number of weeks early your baby was. This will give you the adjusted age.

For example, let's say your baby was born three weeks early. His birthday was seven weeks ago. Even though he's been on the other side of the womb for seven weeks, his adjusted age would be four weeks. That's a big difference!

As you read this book, be sure to reference your child's adjusted age to determine what milestones he or she should be reaching at any given time.

ALL ABOUT APGAR TEST AND SCORES

If you've heard other parents discussing childbirth and delivery, you might have heard them refer to the Apgar test. This is a routine test done right after delivery, in the first minute to be exact. The test is then repeated five minutes later.

Sign	2	1	0
A (Appearance)	Pink body	Pink body, blue fingers/toes	Pale or blue
P (Pulse)	Greater than 100 bpm	Less than 100 bpm	No pulse
G (Grimace)	Crying or coughing	Facial change or weak cry	No response
A (Activity)	Active, moving	Limited movement	No movement
R (Respiration)	Strong cry	Irregular breath	No breathing

Like any scoring system, Apgar scores are limited, but they do give you a good picture of your baby's health after delivery. Here is a chart that shows the five signs the medical team will look for and what score your baby can receive for each.

Your medical team will add up all the signs to score your baby. For example, if your baby got a 1 for appearance, 2 for pulse, 2 for grimace, 1 for activity, and 2 for respiration, the score would be 8.

Generally speaking, a 5-minute Apgar score of 7 and higher is considered satisfactory. If it's lower than that, the medical team will continue taking the score every five minutes and will administer any medications or other interventions as needed.

Keep in mind that even if your baby's 1-minute Apgar score is low, things can turn around quickly. For example, one of our kids was born with a one-minute Apgar of 6, but by the five-minute mark it was up to 10. He's now six years old, super smart, and definitely not lethargic. Some babies just take a little longer than others to perk up!

FIRST-TIME DAD TIPS

Regardless of the type of delivery, here is some seasoned dad advice for the first 24 hours post-delivery:

1. **Sleep, Sleep, Sleep!** Your partner will be sore and exhausted in the first 24 hours after delivery. And of course, you'll also be totally wiped out from supporting her and going through the emotional rollercoaster of childbirth. This is why it's great to have the hospital staff change diapers, check on mom, and do other routine tasks. Take advantage of the help and get as much sleep as you can. Now is not the time to learn the ropes - now is the time to get as much R&R as possible.

2. **Connect:** You and your partner have a lot to talk about, especially if things didn't go the way you planned. Additionally, the first 24 hours is great baby bonding time. Babies love skin-to-skin contact, and science says it's one of the best things for them in the first 24 hours post-birth. A study showed that moms who had immediate skin-to-skin contact with their babies experienced lower rates of postpartum depression and that babies cried less and slept more. That's a win-win! It also has been shown to help premature babies adjust and breastfeed. Dads can definitely do skin-to-skin, too, with the same benefits for baby and extra bonding for the two of you.

It's not often you hear the best thing for you to do is chill out, binge Netflix, and enjoy quality time with your partner - but that's really the best thing for you to do now! So kick back and relax (with your tiny newborn on your chest).

CHAPTER 2
COMING HOME WITH YOUR NEW BABY

THERE ARE a lot of different opinions on the best time to leave the hospital. Some parents are counting down the minutes until they can leave. Others might enjoy the care from medical staff and see it as an extended date night (especially if the hospital food is actually decent!).

Here's what you need to know about when you'll be discharged and how to survive your first few nights at home as a family of three.

LEAVING THE HOSPITAL

The number of days you will spend in the hospital after childbirth varies. For an uncomplicated delivery, you might spend two days in the hospital. For a more complex delivery such as a c-section, it might take four days or more to come home.

Generally, you can expect to spend two to five days in the hospital after delivery, but it could be longer than that, especially if there were any complications surrounding your baby's delivery.

You might find it more helpful to think of your hospital discharge in terms of milestones rather than a number of days. Specifically, these five things need to happen in order for you to bring baby home:

1. Baby Is Feeding Well: Whether your baby is bottle-fed or breast-fed, the hospital staff needs to know that baby is receiving enough nourishment before sending you home. This is why nurses track the number of dirty diapers your baby has. Too few diapers could signal that your baby is not getting enough milk and might need supplementation. Additionally, if mom is struggling to breastfeed, it's best to get things under control before discharge. Most hospitals have lactation consultants on staff who can help with feeding difficulties during your postpartum stay.

2. Tests and Exams Are Complete: Your newborn will have to undergo routine tests and examinations before he or she can be sent home from the hospital. Generally, these will be done in the first 24 hours and might include the following:

- Newborn screen: A routine check for genetic and metabolic disorders such as cystic fibrosis, sickle cell anemia, and congenital heart disease
- Hepatitis B vaccine: Normally given in the first 24 hours after birth
- Newborn examination: Routine check for reflexes, weight, and general physical appearance
- Newborn hearing screen: Routine hearing test to detect any hearing problems

Depending on the circumstances of your baby's delivery, other tests and examinations may be required to ensure your baby gets a strong start at home.

3. Car Seat Has Been Approved: If your baby was born prematurely, most hospitals in the United States will require a car seat safety test before postpartum hospital discharge. This test takes 90 - 120 minutes and must be completed before your baby can be discharged since it ensures he or she will be safe for the car ride home.

4. Mom's Recovery Is On Track: Regardless of how your baby was born, your partner is going through a challenging recovery. Before you can leave the hospital, the staff needs to know her recovery is on track.

If your partner had a cesarean section or experienced heavy bleeding, you might need to spend a few extra days to make sure she's ready to transition out of the hospital.

5. Paperwork Is Complete: No important life event is complete without paperwork, and birth is no exception! You'll need to complete several documents, such as the baby's birth certificate application and Social Security paperwork. Some hospitals also have required classes or reading for new parents that you might have to sign off on before discharge.

While your partner and baby are waiting to leave the hospital, if you have not done so yet, take some time to get the house set up for your baby's trip home. Specifically, here are some things you can do to make sure your first night at home is a smooth transition:

- Tidy Up! New moms need to rest and relax as much as possible, and coming home to messes and chaos doesn't encourage this goal. Make sure the house is clean and in order before you go back home. If you don't feel like you have time to do this yourself, hire a cleaning company to do a thorough clean, or as a friend or family member if they might be able to help.
- Prepare the Sleep Space: Make sure the crib is set up with all the bedding in place, as well as a spare set of sheets.
- Stock the Baby Supplies: Have diapers, wipes, burp cloths, receiving blankets, pacifiers, and other baby gear stocked up and in an accessible location - preferable within arm's reach of your partner's bed, or wherever she plans to rest.
- Stock and Clean the Fridge: Make sure the fridge is stocked with healthy foods you and your partner enjoy. If your partner plans to formula feed or pump breastmilk, set aside some space for bottles.
- Clean and Organize Baby Clothes: Make sure you have a few days of onesies, sleepers, and hats clean for the baby. These should also be put within arm's reach of your partner's sleeping space for easy clothes changes.

- Set Up the Bathroom: Keep an eye on the products your partner is using for recovery in the hospital, such as maxi pads, ice packs, and breast pads. Have a care basket ready for her to keep in the bathroom so she has easy access to her personal needs. To go a step beyond, you can also prepare her a basket of things she can do in bed to stay busy during her recovery period.

GOING HOME

Once your medical team gives the green light, it's discharge time! Here are some things to think about as you plan your first few days home:

Transportation: If you're driving home, take some time to familiarize yourself with the pickup location. Get the car seat installed before you head down to the car with your partner and baby so you can easily transition from the hospital to the car.

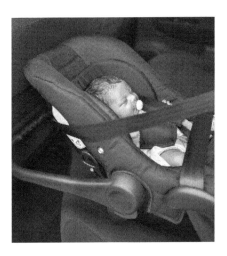

If you depend on someone else for a ride, be mindful of your hospital discharge timeline. Remember that you'll also need to be escorted to the pickup area, which can take a while - so plan accordingly!

Food: You and your partner have both gone through one of the most intense experiences life can throw at you. Make sure you nourish yourselves with healthy foods that you enjoy and are easily prepared. Don't hesitate to reach out to family, friends, and coworkers to see if someone can organize a meal train for you and the family. There are so many websites to easily create weeks of organized meals during this adjustment period - it's very straightforward!

Whether you have a meal train or not, be sure to have a lot of tasty foods on hand. It can be difficult to go to the bathroom after delivery, so high-fiber foods are a great choice. If your partner seems to be craving high-calorie and high-carb food options, this is totally normal.

Provide a variety of foods your partner likes that will get her metabolism going and give her the energy she needs to adjust. Finally, make sure she stays hydrated - a good rule is to always make sure she is drinking water if she's feeding the baby.

Healing: Make sure the environment at home is restful and peaceful. Your partner may be more sensitive to sounds and lighting than usual, which is totally normal. Additionally, it's best to assume mom is not doing any chores for a while. If you need to return to work right away, try to reach out to family and friends in the area to arrange help in the first few weeks, so your partner can focus on resting and bonding with the baby.

Visitors: If you live close to family and friends, you'll probably have people ask if they can visit. Be fearless about saying "no" if you think visitors might hinder the healing process, especially during the first few days at home. Some parents find it helpful to have a list of helpful tasks to give visitors when they come over - for example, asking for help doing a load of dishes or folding a load of laundry. Don't be afraid to ask for assistance!

Communication: Your partner is processing a lot, and she needs support and encouragement. Understand she might seem despondent or negative, and realize this is a normal hormonal transition. Try not to be critical, which will only make her feel alienated.

If you notice signs of postpartum depression, such as mood swings, lack of bonding between your partner and the baby, irrational fears, extreme fatigue, or anything that suggests your partner is having thoughts about self-harm, reach out to a medical professional.

A final note: it's normal for new babies to sleep peacefully in the hospital, only to wake every hour or two once they get home. This is a very common experience, so plan to take turns rocking and walking with your baby throughout the night. If possible, ask a family member, friend, or postpartum doula to help with these first few nights, to allow you and your partner to get some much-needed rest.

YOUR BABY'S BIG 3: FEEDING, CRYING, AND SLEEPING

As excited as you might be to come home from the hospital, you may also have an urgent question: what do I do now? Or more importantly, what should I expect baby to do now that he or she is home?

There are three answers. Your baby will:

1. Eat
2. Cry
3. Sleep

Here's how to meet your newborn's three most fundamental needs.

Feeding

Breastfeeding

Aside from resting and healing, your partner's #1 priority in the first days and weeks postpartum will be to establish a healthy breastfeeding pattern.

That might sound easy, but breastfeeding can actually be a little challenging, especially for first-time moms. Here are some tips to help you help her:

1. **Timing**: Don't worry about a feeding schedule at this point. For the first few weeks, nursing on demand is the best way to establish a healthy milk supply. But naturally, that can be quite demanding! Your partner might feel like she is nursing around the clock. Reassure her that this is normal and will ultimately help her body regulate and provide enough milk for the baby.

2. **Conversation:** Postpartum can be a lonely time, and if your partner is at high risk for postpartum depression, simply taking the time to talk to her while she nurses your baby can be a huge help. Ask how she's doing and what she's feeling. Make it a point to sit down with

her from time to time, just because. It won't go unnoticed and will help her look forward to feeding sessions!

3. Rest: Some new moms have a hard time accepting that they need to rest. If your partner insists on being up and about, encourage her to take frequent breaks. This will allow her to get adequate rest and prevent breastfeeding-associated problems like mastitis.

If you notice your partner struggling with any of the following symptoms, encourage her to discuss them with her doctor or a lactation consultant right away, as they can indicate or lead to a breast infection, or mastitis:

- Bleeding or cracked nipples
- Pain during letdown (when her body releases milk to the baby)
- Swelling or tenderness
- Fever

Bottle feeding

There are a lot of reasons women choose to bottle-feed, including medical concerns, convenience, or job pressures. Just like the decision to breastfeed, your partner needs to know you are on board and support this decision.

You might hear people say you can't bond with your baby if you bottle feed. Evidence suggests this is *not* the case. Additionally, bottle feeding provides a great opportunity for dads to bond with their newborns.

Here are step-by-step instructions to feed your baby a bottle:

1. Prepare your space: Set out a burp cloth, blanket, and anything you might want for yourself at the location you will feed your baby. It's annoying to sit down to feed a newborn and realize you have to get right back up and get something you forgot.

2. Prepare baby: Make sure baby has a clean diaper and is dressed comfortably so he's not fussy during your feeding. If your baby likes being swaddled, this would be a good time to get him all swaddled and cozy (better chances he'll take a snooze that way!).

3. Prepare the bottle: Wash your hands thoroughly, then mix the formula according to the directions on the packaging. Contrary to popular belief, you really don't *have* to warm baby bottles, although your baby might prefer milk that is warm to cold milk straight from the fridge. If you want to warm the milk, you can run the bottle under hot water for a minute or two. Always test the formula on your wrist to make sure it's not too hot. Avoid using the microwave to heat milk, since it can scald the milk.

4. Position baby: This takes some practice, but generally speaking, babies love to be held in a cradle hold position while drinking from a bottle - similar to the breastfeeding position, but slightly more upright. Make sure to support his head and neck. If your baby is prone to dribbling or spitting up, lie a bib under his chin to catch any milk.

5. Get a good latch: Once you have baby settled, take the bottle and tap or rub the nipple lightly on his bottom lip until he opens his mouth. You can also just put the bottle in his mouth, but you'll get a better latch if you encourage him to go for it on his own. The baby's lips should be flared and open around the wide base of the nipple, not just the skinny top part.

6. Position the bottle: Once baby gets a good latch, keep the bottle horizontal at a slight angle. Make sure the milk completely covers the outlet of the nipple, since baby can get gassy if he inhales air.

At this age, babies usually don't take too many breaks when they're eating, but if your baby seems to be overwhelmed, don't hesitate to take a break and burp him for a minute or two before trying to continue.

It's also very normal for babies to fall asleep while taking a bottle. This generally isn't a problem, but if your baby isn't meeting weight gain recommendations, you might need to stimulate him a bit more during feedings to encourage him to finish his bottle. For example, instead of changing the baby's diaper before a feeding, try interrupting the feeding with a diaper change when he starts to nod off.

How to Burp a Baby

Once your baby is done with a feeding, it's important to burp the baby. This prevents gas from building up in your baby's tummy, which can cause abdominal cramping and discomfort. There are a lot of different ways to burp your baby, but these are my favorite positions:

1. **The Classic**: Hold baby upright with his head on your shoulder. Gently thump his back to release air bubbles.
2. **Sit-up Style**: This position is best when your baby has a bit of head control. Sit baby up on your knee and pat his back in this position.
3. **Netflix Style:** The classic position to use while you're watching your favorite show. Place baby tummy down across your knees, making sure his head is to the side, then burp away.

Regardless of the position, make sure you have a burp cloth in place in case baby spits up, which is pretty common at this age! When you burp the baby, don't pat her back in the same position the whole time. I like to alternate between patting, rubbing in circles, and rubbing up and down her back to get the air moving.

Supplements

For the most part, breastmilk or baby formula provide all the calories and nutrients your baby needs. However, there are a few supplements doctors recommend for the first month of your baby's life:

Vitamin D: If your baby is exclusively or partially breastfed, most pediatricians recommend supplementing vitamin D. This important vitamin helps baby develop a robust immune system and prevents rickets. Formula is often fortified with vitamin D, but breastmilk does not contain very much. The other natural source of vitamin D is direct sunlight, which doctors recommend limiting for newborns, so supplements can help make up for any deficiencies. The drops are easy to add to a bottle or some expressed breastmilk.

Iron: Usually babies don't need iron supplementation until they are a bit older, but if your baby was premature or born with low birth weight, your pediatrician might recommend an iron supplement.

Aside from these supplements, you probably won't have to supplement your baby's diet of breastmilk and formula. Water and juice are too hard on the baby's stomach at this stage of development.

Reading Your Baby's Cry

Crying is your baby's sole means of communication, and while it might seem like crying is crying, that's not actually the case. If you listen carefully, you can hear different types of cries, and each one communicates something different.

Through the years, child development experts have worked out a way to decode a baby's cry. One theory, put forth by a woman named Priscilla Dunston, suggests that babies all make similar sounds right *before* they start crying. Those sounds are:

Sound	Translation
"Neh"	I need food!
"Eh"	I need help releasing gas (burping!)
"Eaaarrrgh"	I need to poop!
"Heh"	I'm too warm/too cold!
"Owh"	I need sleep!

Listening for these sounds is a good way to give your baby what he or she needs before the crying begins. But if you've missed that window of opportunity, there are also many theories about the different cries babies have in the first months of life. For example, some cries just sound like complaining, whereas others sound like your baby is in pain.

A Google search for "how many kinds of cries do babies have" returns some confusing and even conflicting results. I find it easiest to break newborn cries into 4 categories:

1. **Crying from hunger:** This cry sounds angry and growl-like (seriously!). Just like with the different kinds of sounds before crying, it might start with a "n" sound. Child development experts suggest this is because when newborns nurse, the tongue comes in contact with the roof of the mouth, and this cry mimics that physiological response. Whatever the scientific reason, this cry sounds like "I'm angry you're

not feeding me – feed me now!" The obvious response: get the bottle ASAP (or find mom!).

2. **Crying from gas:** This is an unmistakeable, high-pitched scream/cry. It might come in spurts, as opposed to the hunger cries which are more long-winded. You might also notice the baby's face becoming red or that the baby is scrunching up his or her legs. That's a classic gas-relieving posture, and indicates your little guy or gal is having some serious gas. You can help by burping your baby, pumping his or her legs to relieve cramping, or just walking while patting the baby's back and "shushing", which is a soothing sound for newborns.

3. **Crying from discomfort:** This cry is similar to the grumpy hunger cry. If baby doesn't seem hungry or gassy, the crying could be discomfort related to body temperature or a dirty diaper. Start by checking the diaper and seeing if baby needs a change (more on how to do that in a bit!), then feel his or her fingers, ears, and toes to see if you need to swaddle or put on socks or a hat. Or if baby seems too warm, a little skin-to-skin on dad's chest is just the fix!

4. **Crying from exhaustion**: Your baby might just need a nap. If you've had a lot of people over to visit, or recently taken a trip out of the house, he or she could be overstimulated. Go to a quiet room, dim the lights, and walk with the baby while "shushing" and rocking in a rhythmic motion. Again, if you can do this with baby skin-to-skin, even better!

So how much do newborns cry, anyways? I hate to be the bearer of bad news, but they usually cry a lot. In the first six weeks, it's totally normal for a baby to cry got two or three hours per day. Some of that crying is simple to fix, and some of it is unexplained. If your baby has colic, it's normal for him or her to cry 3+ hours.

The most important thing to remember is that at this age, it's best to respond to a crying baby. You might hear some people say picking up a crying newborn will "spoil" him or her, but nothing could be further from the truth. Responding to your baby's cry promptly and taking the time to figure out what's wrong is one of the first ways you establish trust. Put simply, a newborn crying is *not* the same as a toddler throwing a tantrum. So if your immediate instinct is to provide assistance, trust that intuition.

On the other hand, if your immediate instinct is *not* to provide assistance because you're absolutely exhausted, that's also normal! Having a plan in place to take shifts with your partner is crucial here. If your baby has colic, asking a family member for help or hiring a postpartum doula can also be a tremendous help.

Finally, remember this stage doesn't last forever. Your baby is going through huge changes right now, but once things regulate, it gets better. I promise!

Helping Your Baby Sleep

Sleep Training and Schedules

Sleep training and schedules are lifesavers…when your baby is older. For the newborn stage, it's best to try to sleep when baby sleeps as much as you can. Most newborns are only awake for 7-10 hours per day, so that's not a bad deal!

It's totally normal for your newborn to have his or her days and nights mixed up, especially in the first week after you come home from the hospital. The best way to cope with this is to simply clear your schedule as much as possible and plan for a week of down-time. The more you can go with the baby's flow, the more rest you'll get.

The bottom line: for now, skip the schedules.

The "Family Bed"

Along with politics and religion, the subject "baby sleeping arrangements" belongs on the list of things *not* to discuss at holiday gatherings.

Before I had kids, I swore I would *never* have a family bed situation. Not only was I raised to believe it was dangerous, but it also seemed like a total invasion of privacy. But as with many things to do with parenting, I've become a bit less dogmatic through the years. And I'm not

alone: a study showed that parents in the United States increasingly report that they have a family bed situation during the first three months postpartum.

Now if someone asks me about my perspective on the family bed, my answer is: it depends.

More specifically, there are two important factors to consider if you're trying to figure out whether a family bed option is for you:

1. **Safety**: Just like a non-family bed situation, safety is of utmost importance if you decide to co-sleep. Here are some non-negotiables for bed sharing:

- Never sleep with your baby on a couch, sofa, or armchair. The safest place is a king-size bed to give baby plenty of space.
- Don't surround your baby with pillows, sheets, blankets, stuffed animals, or any other objects that might be able to accidentally cover his or her face. My partner and I co-slept with two of our babies who had a hard time sleeping separately. During this time, we slept on either side of baby in a king-sized bed. We both used separate bedding (twin sheets and a light blanket), and just a small pillow. This way, baby had plenty of space to sleep in the middle of the bed.
- Never co-sleep with your baby if you have had any kind of medication that affects sleep, alcohol, or cigarettes. It's not worth it the risk. If mom is still taking painkillers from delivery, it's best for the baby to sleep in a separate space to avoid the risk of suffocation.
- If your baby was born premature or weighs less than 5.5 lb, experts recommend you skip the family bed until baby is older.
- Always place baby on his or her back to sleep. Research shows that at this stage, sleeping in a supine position greatly reduces the chances of SIDS.

2. **Sanity**: If bed-sharing causes sleepless nights and stress dreams, don't do it! Likewise, if you and mom sleep better with your baby close by, the added hours of sleep (and therefore parental sanity) might be worth it, as long as all the safety precautions are in place.

If the idea of a family bed isn't quite up your alley, consider room-sharing. Room-sharing is sleeping with your baby in the same room, with a co-sleeper crib or bassinet set up right next to your bed. It's almost like your baby's in bed with you.

This is my personal preference because it provides the advantages of the family bed (helps baby regulate, encourages breastfeeding, and is just more convenient), but allows me to sleep more at ease and not worry about whether I'm going to roll too close to baby, throw my blanket over him, etc.

Finally, perhaps the most important factor is communicating with your partner. Whatever sleeping arrangement you choose, it's important for you both to be on the same page. That might involve some give-and-take on both sides, but it's definitely best to make the decision together.

SIDS

SIDS (sudden infant death syndrome) is defined as an infant death that occurs in a previously healthy infant, for unknown reasons, during the sleep cycle. I know people personally who have gone through this, and it's a scary thing to think about as a new dad.

There are still so many things we don't know about SIDS, but research has shown a correlation between three risk factors (known as the Triple Risk Model) and SIDS occurrence:

1. Infant vulnerability

2. Baby's period of development (the most critical stage is defined as 2-4 months of age) 3. Environmental stressors (soft bedding, cigarette smoking during pregnancy, unsafe co-sleeping, etc.)

Some exciting research released in 2022 suggested that babies with decreased amounts of an enzyme called butyrylcholinesterase might be at higher risk for SIDS, but the exact causes remain unknown. Until we know more, following safe sleep recommendations, especially with vulnerable infants and those between 2-4 months of age, is the best way to prevent SIDS.

Additionally, the American Academy of Pediatrics recommends sleeping in the same room as your baby for at least the first six months of life. Room sharing allows your baby to regulate his or her sleep by tuning into you and your partner's breathing patterns. Pretty amazing! And of course, that works both ways. You'll be able to keep a watchful eye on the baby if he or she is close to your bed.

Remember, everyone's getting the hang of things in these first few days, so don't get discouraged! Think of this time as the "getting to know you" period. As the days go on you'll start to get a sense for your baby's preferences, which hopefully means more sleep for you and your partner.

CHAPTER 3
BABY CARE 101

SO YOU'VE MADE it home and are adjusting to a good eating and sleeping rhythm. Now it's time to level up!

Newborns are actually pretty low maintenance in the first weeks. They might go through a challenging adjustment period when you first arrive home, but once things settle down, they basically just sleep, eat, and poop.

But still, it's a huge change for most couples, and you might feel a little in over your head. Here are some tips for six of the most fundamental baby care needs to help you get your footing:

1. Swaddling
2. Changing diapers
3. Holding the baby
4. Bathing
5. Clothing
6. Basic healthcare

SWADDLING

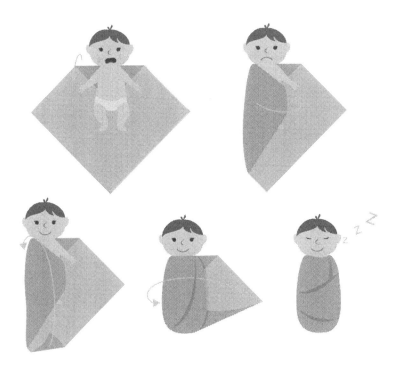

Along with "side/stomach", "shush", "swing", and "suck", "swaddle" is one of the famous "5 S's" of infant care put forth by Dr. Harvey Karp, author of the bestselling book *Happiest Baby on the Block*. Why does swaddling have such a mesmerizing effect on babies?

Well, if you think about the way your baby has spent the first nine months of his or her existence - hanging out in mom's womb, in a constricted, warm, comforting environment - it makes a lot of sense! Swaddling simply mimics the baby's initial, familiar environment.

Swaddling your baby may seem daunting, but it's really simple. Nevertheless, I highly recommend practicing with a baby doll the first few times to get the hang of it.

. . .

Swaddling Your Baby Step-by-Step

1. Fold a swaddling blanket in half so that it forms a triangle (corner to corner), and place it on a soft, open surface like your bed.
2. Lie baby right in the middle.
3. Fold the top right (or left, it doesn't really matter) corner down across the baby's right shoulder and left hip/upper thigh. Tuck it behind baby. You'll have a little bit remaining at the bottom - that's fine.
4. Tuck the little bit remaining at the bottom under the baby's left shoulder.
5. Repeat step 3 with the other side.
6. Tuck any remaining blanket in at baby's chest.

It's that simple! From here, simply pick your baby up and do some of those other 5 S's for ultimate soothing superpowers.

You might wonder whether swaddling is safe for your newborn. A 2014 study in the *Journal of Pediatrics* investigated several cases of SIDS to try to answer that question. According to the research team, instances of SIDS did not seem to be related to swaddling but rather to unsafe sleep conditions (such as baby sleeping on his tummy instead of his back) and items such as bumpers and soft bedding. So rest assured, swaddling is safe and effective.

CHANGING DIAPERS

Ah, diapers: commonly known as the bane of every dad's existence. But it doesn't have to be this way! Changing diapers is a simple process as long as you have a strategy.

Before you do the deed, you'll need to prepare your space. This means putting some kind of non-precious surface (often a disposable changing pad, but it could also be a paper towel or clean towel) under your baby *before* you begin the diaper-changing process. Additionally, have plenty of wipes (5+ for poopy diapers or 2+ for wet diapers), as well as a few extra diapers close by. Finally, if you're dealing with any kind of baby diaper rash, have your diaper cream of choice open and ready nearby.

Here's a step-by-step breakdown to help you conquer the ultimate dad task. The first few times might be a little slow, but eventually, you'll pick up speed, especially with a properly prepared space. This is important because the longer the process takes, the more likely you are to 1.) upset your adorable baby and 2.) have to change your shirt.

Changing Your Baby Step-by-Step:

1. Lie baby down on your changing table or another surface.
2. Undress the baby down to the diaper.
3. Place the clean diaper under the diaper you are about to change. This is important because there's a very good chance

your baby will eliminate pee or poop as soon as you open that diaper. Be prepared!

4. Unfasten the dirty diaper and pull the front down toward the baby's feet while gently bending his legs and bringing his feet up toward the belly. This is your first peek at what's in that diaper. Grab wipes accordingly.

5. Gently clean your baby's diaper area. For girls, be sure to wipe from front to back to avoid infection. There are a lot of crevices down there, so be careful to clean thoroughly! When you've finished, remove the old diaper from under your baby.

6. Quickly inspect the diaper area for any rashes or irritation. If your baby is developing a rash, it's important to wait a little while and allow the skin to dry. I know it seems like an eternity, but it will help prevent the rash from worsening.

7. Apply the diaper cream of your choice once the skin is dry, and gently clean the umbilical cord with a clean baby wipe.

8. Put the new diaper on. If your baby's umbilical stump hasn't fallen off, you can just fold the top of the diaper down so the belly button has room to breathe.

9. Tidy up. This step is the icing on the cake because it's where you will really impress your partner. Don't get me wrong - it's impressive enough that you're changing diapers to begin with. But by throwing any dirty clothes in the laundry and making sure to put the diaper in the appropriate disposal bin, you'll go a step beyond.

That's a wrap. Your baby might be pretty angry at this point - totally normal. Redress the baby and take a little walk to calm him down.

FAQs About Diaper Changes

1. **How many diapers per day?** Your baby will have 10 - 12 dirty (wet or poopy) diapers per day. Yes, this means every two hours, on average. Additionally, your baby might pee or poop

at unexpected moments. Yes, that might be when you remove the previous diaper and are most vulnerable. Accepting this fact will allow you to be calm and collected when it happens.

2. **What causes diaper rashes?** There are a few things that can cause diaper rashes. In the first week after birth, your baby's skin might just be extra sensitive. A lot of new babies develop minor rashes that resolve as they adjust.

3. **Do I need diaper cream?** It's helpful to have a few diaper creams on hand just in case your baby develops a rash. However, there are a few other ways you can prevent rashes before they become a problem. The first is to change your baby regularly. Poopy diapers should be changed as soon as possible to avoid irritating the skin. Keeping your baby's bottom clean and dry is key. Second, as scary as it sounds, giving your baby's bottom some air time after each change will also go a long way in preventing rashes.

4. **What kind of diaper cream is best?** This is a hotly debated issue, but the answer really depends on your baby's skin and the cause of the diaper rash. Generally speaking, diaper creams that contain zinc oxide will do a great job of clearing up an already-existing rash. But if you're looking for prevention rather than treatment, all you really need is a barrier to keep your baby's bum from getting too moist and developing a rash. These products are often called "ointments," "balms" or "healing creams."

5. **When should I worry about a diaper rash?** A diaper rash that causes open sores, extreme discomfort, or prolonged symptoms warrants a trip to the doctor. Your doctor may be able to prescribe a stronger cream to clear up the rash.

6. **What kind of diapers and wipes should I buy?** There are so many diapers and wipes on the market, so selecting the one you want to use can be overwhelming. Our kids have done best with unscented wipes and diapers that are designed for babies with sensitive skin, especially during the newborn period. But, like so many other parenting decisions, trial and error is the best teacher here.

7. **What about cloth diapers?** Cloth diapering has become much
    more popular and manageable in recent years. Gone are the
    days of giant diaper pins and boiling diapers to sanitize them.
    Today's cloth diapers are designed to be convenient and cute.
    That said, it's still quite the undertaking. We cloth-diapered
    three of our kids but waited until we got the hang of it to start
    right away. If you plan to use cloth diapers, it can be a little less
    stressful to have disposables on hand, just in case you aren't
    quite ready to jump into it immediately.

HOLDING YOUR BABY

It's amazing how intimidating holding a newborn can be. But study
after study shows that babies who are held - ideally skin-to-skin -
adjust better to life outside the womb.

I remember being slightly terrified to hold our first baby. She was so
tiny and looked like a breakable baby doll. Plus, she was covered in
vernix (that white waxy stuff a lot of newborns are born with), which
kind of freaked me out. Of course, eventually I conquered my fear and
also realized newborns aren't nearly as fragile as they appear.

What's the best way to pick up your newborn? It's hard to give step-
by-step instructions, since you're always picking up or being handed

the baby at different angles. Let's go through the classic 4 W's and 1 H ("Where, What, When, Why, How?") to touch on some important points to keep in mind when you hold your little one.

Where: Your baby feels most stable when you support their most wobbly points: namely, their head (and neck) and legs.

What: Keep in mind what holding is, especially in this first month: an imitation of the mother's womb. Based on that image, it makes sense why making shushing noises and rocking the baby would help soothe him.

When: Clue into your baby's cues to determine if now is the time to be held or do something else (feeding, diaper change, etc.). I remember feeling personally offended when my baby didn't want to be held, only to later realize it was because I hadn't really taken the time to check in with my partner about the last time the baby had eaten or been changed.

Why: Being held is, first and foremost, an act of bonding. It's easy to forget when kids are newborns, but try to remember that those hours you spend holding your baby are establishing a relationship of trust --- *for life.*

How: Be relaxed. Babies can be oddly intimidating, but if you take a deep breath (inhale and exhale) before picking your baby up, you're less likely to tense up and make your baby feel squished or stressed. Dads have been holding babies since the dawn of humanity - you've got this!

And don't forget the amazing benefits of holding your baby skin-to-skin. For example, a study found that newborns who were born via c-section and were held skin-to-skin (by dad) cried significantly less than those who were placed in a cot. The babies who received skin-to-skin contact with dad and were held on his chest cried for an average of 60 minutes after delivery. Babies who were placed in a cot cried for an average of 110 minutes - almost twice as long!

The research team concluded: "The infants in the skin-to-skin group were comforted; that is, they stopped crying, became calmer, and reached a drowsy state earlier than the infants in the cot group."

It's totally normal for your newborn not to like being held in any position that vaguely resembles their nursing position, including the popular cradle hold. If being cradled isn't your baby's thing, there are a lot of other ways to hold your baby. Here are two of my favorites:

The Football Hold: This is a holding position many dads (including myself) love: the football hold. In this hold, you support the baby beneath the chest, neck, and head, as well as the legs, so that baby is head down on his or her tummy across your forearm. His head should be nestled in the crook of your elbow. Holding your baby in this position often relieves gas, which is why it's often considered a great hold for colicky babies.

Over-the-Shoulder Hold: This one is exactly what it sounds like - holding baby upright, looking over one of your shoulders. This is a classic holding position that's great for burping your baby. Just make sure you have a burp cloth under the baby. Eventually, your baby will hold his or her

head up in this position, but for now, be sure to provide support for the head and neck, which can be a bit unstable at this age.

BATHING YOUR BABY

The skin is the body's largest organ, so it makes sense that a lot of newborns go through some major skin changes in the first week or two after birth. It's totally normal for newborns to have baby acne, dry skin, and blemishes. Keeping your baby's skin clean is the best way to prevent these normal occurrences from becoming more serious problems.

Bathing Your Baby Step-by-Step:

1. **Gather your supplies:** Grab your baby shampoo, four washcloths, a few diapers, baby wipes, a baby brush, a nail file/emery board, and a towel. Get two of the washcloths slightly wet and apply a squirt of baby shampoo, then rub the fabric together to get a lather. Keep the other two soap-free, but dampen them with room-temperature water.

2. **Prepare the bath water:** Make sure the water is just a bit warmer than room temperature (around 99 degrees Fahrenheit but not hot. Whether you're using a baby bathtub, a regular bath, or a sink, you don't need a lot of water. A couple of inches will do just fine.

3. **Undress baby.** Don't do this before you prepare the water, or your baby might get too cold. If you're worried about your baby pooping in the tub, it's totally fine to keep the diaper on until the very end.

4. **Place baby in the water.** Support her head and neck with one hand, and bottom and legs with the other. Talk to her with a calm voice as you do this to reassure her it's okay and that you're there.

5. **Bathe your baby's body:** With the soapy washcloth, gently clean your baby from the neck all the way to the toes. If you left her diaper on, you can remove it to clean the diaper area.

6. **Wash your baby's head/hair:** Gently wash your baby's head with the second soapy washcloth. Be careful with the soft spot - you really don't have to apply pressure. This is just to remove some of the oils from the baby's head to minimize cradle cap, which is caused by oil buildup on the baby's scalp.

7. **Remove excess soap:** With the third washcloth, wipe off any excess soap on the baby's body, then do the same on the baby's head with the fourth washcloth. (I like to use a separate washcloth to wash and rinse the baby's head to avoid passing any germs from the diaper area.)

8. **Wrap baby in a towel and take her out of the bath.** Gently dry your baby off, then put on a fresh diaper and clothes.

9. **File baby's nails if needed.** Some parents like to use nail clippers, but I prefer a small emery board. They make them in baby sizes, but you can also use a regular one or even a nail file. Gently file baby's nails down - they grow quickly, and since newborns don't have great fine motor skills yet, it's common for them to scratch their faces!

If your partner or someone else can help with bath time, it's nice to have a second pair of hands. If not, there's another way you can do it that's much simpler: a sponge bath. You don't need to do it in the bathtub or other tub - you can just wipe baby down with a clean, wet washcloth (same temperature of water) and a tiny bit of baby soap if desired. Just make sure to have a clean towel underneath the baby, some warm blankets, and plenty of diapers and wipes close by.

CLOTHING YOUR BABY

Newborns really don't need a lot of clothes. My partner and I have six kids, and through the years we've managed to get this down to a science. Here's a "bare essentials" wardrobe for the first few weeks:

- 5 footed sleepers
- 5 daytime onesies (long or short sleeves, depending on the temperature) • 5 nighttime onesies (long sleeves preferable)
- 3 sleep sacks
- 5 pairs of footed pants
- 7 pairs of socks
- 5 baby hats
- 5 swaddle blankets

Here's a bit of info about each item and why I consider them essential:

Footed sleepers: These are great for taking the baby to doctor appointments or other outings. You don't have to worry about socks (although you can certainly still put them on under the sleeper), and they are easy to put on and take off.

Onesies: The classic baby clothing item. Onesies are great because the snaps keep them in place. A tip for diaper blowouts: most onesies have shoulders you can open to pull the onesie *down* and off the baby, instead of *up* and over the baby's head. Better to keep the poop contained in baby's bottom half than to risk any head involvement!

Sleep sacks: These look kind of like giant baby sleeping bags, which is basically what they are. Sleep sacks are great because they give your baby freedom of motion while sleeping. Our babies have slept well with a long-sleeved onesie underneath.

Footed pants: Footed pants are easy to put on your baby and don't require any socks.

Socks: I have a love/hate relationship with newborn socks. They definitely seem to make babies more comfortable, but they're also always getting lost. Still, if your baby will sleep better with socks on, it's definitely worth it to have several pairs.

Hats: Babies lose a lot of heat through their heads, so having several baby hats is important. Plus, they're really cute.

Swaddle blankets: I consider these a wardrobe item because our babies love being swaddled. Some babies don't, but the beauty of swaddle blankets is you can also use them as regular blankets, burp cloths, nursing coverups for your partner, etc. Choose blankets that are made out of muslin or other natural fibers since these tend to be more breathable and won't cause overheating.

Of course, this is only the bare minimum, and hopefully, you're not doing a ton of laundry, so having more clothing on hand certainly won't hurt. But if you're looking to just get the essentials, this wardrobe should have you covered.

BASIC HEALTHCARE

Taking Your Baby's Temperature

The American Academy of Pediatrics recommends taking newborn temperatures either rectally (I know, not what you want to read!). Other methods just aren't as accurate. But don't worry, it's really not as horrible as it sounds.

Taking Baby's Temperature Step-by-Step

1. Prep the thermometer by wiping it clean with rubbing alcohol. Put a bit of petroleum jelly or coconut oil on the end.
2. Lie baby face down on a soft surface or your lap. It's easiest if he is just wearing a diaper, maybe with a blanket over him if

he seems cold. Pat his back and calm him, so he is relaxed, which will make the process much easier!

3. Gently place your non-dominant hand across the baby's lower back while removing one side of his diaper with your other hand. Pull the diaper back and gently place the thermometer end into the rectal opening - about ½ inch is all. Press the thermometer button and hold the thermometer in place. Keep your other hand on the baby's back and talk to him to reassure him everything is okay. Can't blame him for being a little out of sorts!

4. Wait for the beep, then read the thermometer. Put the diaper back on.

That's it! Newborn temperatures should be less than 100.4 degrees Fahrenheit. If your baby has a fever, contact the pediatrician right away.

Visiting the Pediatrician

Your newborn will need to go in for several doctor visits in the first year of life, and a lot of them take place during the first month. These visits are usually pretty straightforward. Your doctor will ask about feeding, sleeping, and any concerns you have, and will check the baby's length, weight, and head circumference to start a growth chart.

Your baby will also receive his or her second hepatitis B vaccination in the first month (the first one is usually administered at birth).

Here's a typical list of your baby's pediatrician visits for the first year of life:

- Birth
- 3-5 Days After Birth
- 1 Month
- 2 Months
- 4 Months

- 6 Months
- 9 Months
- 12 Months

As your baby grows, the pediatrician will ask more questions relating to language development and motor skills.

Mastering these six skills (swaddling, changing diapers, holding the baby, clothing the baby, giving baby a bath, and doing basic health care tasks) covers most of the bases. Before you know it, you'll be wearing your baby to work! Okay, maybe not, but mastering the basics is really all you need to focus on right now.

Common Illnesses and How to Treat Them

Infants younger than three months should not have over-the-counter medications like Tylenol or Advil without consulting your pediatrician. This can make it hard to know what to do when your baby comes down with a cold or other illness. Here are some simple ways to deal with common health concerns at this age:

- **Fever**: See your pediatrician as soon as possible. Until you can get in, keep baby's temperature down with cool washcloths on the forehead, light clothing, and frequent nursing if you are breastfeeding.
- **Cough**: Use a humidifier for a dry cough, or sit in the bathroom with the hot water on for a few minutes to help loosen chest congestion. Observe your baby and see your pediatrician or urgent care immediately if baby seems like she is struggling to breathe. Keep your baby upright as much as possible.
- **Stuffy Nose**: Use saline nose drops, followed by a nasal aspirator to help clear baby's nose. The NoseFrida is another option a lot of parents love at this age. Again, keeping the baby upright is also helpful.

- **Dry Skin:** Use a fragrance-free moisturizer after bath time. If the air in your house is dry, a humidifier can help here, too.
- **Eye Discharge:** Gently wipe baby's eye from the nose to the outside corner with a piece of clean gauze soaked in warm water.
- **Vomiting:** Focus on keeping baby hydrated. If vomiting continues for more than 24 hours, or if your baby shows signs of dehydration such as crying without tears or cracked lips, consult your pediatrician.
- **Gas:** Try gripe water (only after baby is one month old - be sure to read the label).
- **Cradle Cap:** My favorite remedy for cradle cap is coconut oil. During your baby's bath, gently massage some coconut oil into her scalp (avoid her soft spot!). Then gently brush her head and watch the cradle cap miraculously disappear!

FINDING CHILDCARE

Now that you are home and adjusting to life with your new baby, you're probably thinking about the next big adjustment on the horizon: going back to work. For parents who both work full-time, that also means looking for the right childcare arrangement for your baby.

Here are some questions to ask yourself as you search for the best childcare solution for your family:

1. Do I need part-time or full-time care?
2. Do I prefer an in-home daycare, a nanny who comes to watch the baby at our house, or a traditional daycare?
3. Do I have any family members or friends who might be interested in providing childcare?
4. What specific hours do I need childcare?
5. What is our monthly budget for childcare?

In addition to answering these questions, ask family and friends for recommendations to start out on your search for childcare. Visit each potential childcare provider in person before making any commitments. Finding a trusted daycare, nanny, or other childcare provider to care for your baby is one of the best ways to make the transition back to the workplace as seamless and stress-free as possible.

CHAPTER 4
YOUR BABY'S FIRST MONTH

 "After waiting for long 9 months, I'm finally relaxed and happy to become a proud daddy of a little angel."
—Unknown

THE FIRST MONTH of your baby's life is definitely a rollercoaster, but it's also an amazing and transformative time. I remember telling my partner after our first child was born that I felt the whole experience had pushed me beyond all the limits I thought I had. Not only did I realize I'm actually way more patient and perseverant than I thought, but it also showed me how much love I was capable of giving. You need a lot of love to deal with poopy diapers and sleepless nights.

Hopefully, you have a totally clear calendar and can enjoy these first four weeks. My number one tip: take advantage of the downtime and enjoy transitioning to life as a family of three. Here's what you need to know about your baby, your partner, and dad life this month.

Your Baby's Milestones: Month 1			
Eating	Sleeping	Motor Skills	Language
Eats about 32 ounces per day Takes 3-4 ounces per feeding Breastfeeds every 2 to 3 hours	Sleeps an average of 14 hours per day Sleeps on his or her back	Learns to suckle at the breast of drink from a bottle Still has newborn reflexes such as startle, rooting, stepping, and grasping reflex	Basically just grunts and cries

FEEDING

If you feel like your newborn eats a lot during the first month of life, you're right. Newborns go through rapid changes, and they need that nutrition to provide support. Here are a few considerations for your baby's feeding needs in the first month outside the womb.

Bottle Feeding: Your baby will gradually increase the amount of milk taken each day throughout the first four weeks, and by the end of the first month, she will consume about 32 ounces of milk each day. Expect the baby to take about 3-4 ounces per feeding, although this can vary. The most important number is how much your baby consumes over the course of a day.

You might be heading back to work during this first month, so now is a great time to discuss feeding responsibilities with your partner. A lot of bottle-feeding families like to have set feedings for dad to bond with the baby and give mom a break. If your partner plans to go back to work, this is especially important. For example, taking over a night-time feed is a great way to not only bond with the baby but also help your partner during this recovery stage.

Breastfeeding: If your partner is exclusively breastfeeding, it can be hard to gauge how much milk the baby receives, but if your partner nurses every 2 to 3 hours, this should equate to 32 ounces. Just as with the first few days in the hospital, your baby's output is the best way to tell if the milk supply is adequate, so keep those diapers coming.

A month might seem like plenty of time for your partner to get the hang of breastfeeding, but it's very common for first-time moms to take several months to really feel comfortable with nursing. Not only that, but during this first month, your partner will also still be recovering from childbirth.

Depending on the length of maternity leave, your partner may start feeling anxious about breastfeeding and returning to work. If she is returning to work soon - or if she feels overwhelmed with on-demand breastfeeding - now is a good time to start pumping. Most hospitals will rent out breast pumps for new moms, so discuss this with your doctor.

Remind your partner that she doesn't need to worry too much about output at this point. Breastfeeding on its own is challenging enough, and it can also take a while to get the hang of pumping. She should start with one pumping session in the morning when milk supply is highest, then gradually add in sessions.

SLEEPING

If there's one thing to be grateful for during your newborn's first month, it's that he will sleep a lot. Don't worry about sleep schedules at this point - just try to rest and sleep when your newborn sleeps.

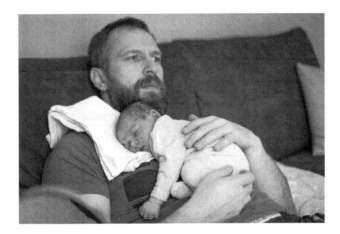

This first month is also a great time to get a feel for your own parenting sleep style. Some parents struggle to sleep with the baby next to the bed, for example, while others can't sleep if they aren't within arm's reach of the baby.

One study suggests that mothers who breastfeed tend to sleep better with baby close by, so keep this in mind if your partner is nursing. The same study found that newborns slept an average of 14 hours per day, regardless of whether they were bottle-fed or breastfed. So take advantage of that time to get some shut-eye!

BONDING WITH BABY

The word "bonding" might summon up saccharine images of dads and newborns gazing lovingly into each other's eyes - and this might not quite capture the entirety of your experience as a new dad. But bonding is so much more than a lovey-dovey activity that makes you and your baby feel good. Study after study has shown that bonding is *biologically necessary* for your baby's growth and well-being - and even for your own.

"When fathers are more engaged in caring for their babies, they experience stronger hormonal and neurobiological changes than when not engaged. These changes are, in turn, associated with short and longer-term benefits for the baby." (Fisher, 2018)

"Fathers have innate biologically-based abilities to bond with and care for babies; these are especially important for the health and safety of babies in situations of stress and risk." (Fisher, 2018)

These are direct quotes from a study published in the *Journal of Neonatal Nursing*. Researchers studied the effects of paternal care on high-risk infants in a neonatal unit. They found that the babies who interacted with dad regularly gained more weight and took to breastfeeding more easily than those who did not.

This is just one instance of evidence that bonding with your newborn helps your baby adjust to being outside the womb.

LEARNING

Believe it or not, the first lesson your baby will learn - and perhaps his most challenging - happens this month. This is the fundamental lesson all human beings have to learn in order to survive: how to consume food.

It's easy to take this for granted but think about the life your baby has had up to this point. She's been floating around in mom's uterus without a care in the world, receiving everything she needs to grow without having to fight for it. What a life!

And then suddenly in that event we call "birth," everything changes. Now she has to work for everything. Her surroundings are completely changed. She feels the air on her skin and sees light for the first time. Her food is no longer magically transported into her body via the umbilical cord. Now she has to work for it.

Learning to eat is your baby's big task this month. It might sound crazy, but your most important task as dad is just to make sure she eats. Walking will come in time.

KEEPING BABY SAFE

Newborns don't move very much, so take advantage of this month and do some childproofing around your house (if you haven't already!). These projects include:

- Checking all smoke and carbon monoxide detectors to make sure they work or installing new ones if necessary
- Reset the water heater to no more than 120 degrees Fahrenheit to avoid making baby bath water too hot
- Check bookshelves and other heavy furniture to make sure it's anchored to the wall (you'll be glad you did this when your baby is pulling up on things!)
- Put baby-proofing plugs in electrical outlets. Again, this won't be a concern for a while, but might as well get a head start!

The most important baby-proofing item on your checklist should be to make sure your newborn sleeps safely. Remove any excess pillows, blankets, or stuffed animals from your baby's crib, bassinet, or other sleeping space. Make sure there are no gaps between the mattress and the frame and that all screws are secured.

HOW IS MOM?

Your partner might start to feel antsy around three weeks postpartum (if not sooner!). Reassure her that taking this time to relax, sleep as much as possible, and bond with your baby will help her bounce back faster in the long run. Study after study has shown this to be the case!

For example, a 2021 study on active-duty Army moms found that taking an extra six weeks (twelve weeks total) to recover from childbirth had the same level of physical fitness as Army moms who only took six weeks off.

You would think that at such an elite level of physical fitness, every week missed would count. But on the contrary, moms who allowed their bodies 12 weeks to recover matched the moms who took off six weeks and even *exceeded* their performance in several areas.

The takeaway? Women who took 12 weeks of maternity leave, as opposed to 6 weeks, did *not* demonstrate lower fitness scores one year postpartum when compared with those who took less time - and in some areas, their scores were better!

Rest is easier said than done, though, and it's easy to overdo it at this stage. Here are a few concerns your partner might have in this first month, and how to respond to them:

1. **Concerns about bleeding:** It's very normal for bleeding to last 4-6 weeks, or even longer. If your partner passes any large clots or feels like she is passing an abnormally high amount of blood, be sure to consult her physician.

2. **Concerns about low milk supply/baby's weight gain:** Again, new moms often fear they're not producing enough milk. Remind your partner of the baby's tiny tummy size (about the size of a large egg at this stage).

3. **Concerns about c-section incision:** Your partner might still be very sore if she had a c-section, and she might feel anxious about infection or other problems with her incision. It might also be hard for her to breastfeed comfortably. Encourage her to rest as much as possible and give it time. My partner loved using a breastfeeding pillow after her c-sections to help provide support while nursing.

4. **Concerns about pain:** If your partner is used to muscling through every illness or discomfort, she might feel annoyed about the need for pain relief. Most women use pain medication like ibuprofen or acetaminophen for the first few weeks postpartum or even longer if they had a complicated delivery. Your partner can also try other pain relief tricks, like a hot water bottle, heating pad, or - even better - a gentle massage from dad.

5. **Concerns about being "good enough":** A lot of first-time parents struggle with that nagging feeling that they just don't

know enough to be a good mom or dad. If your partner is having a challenging recovery, this is even more likely. Try to find opportunities to compliment her and give her positive feedback. The words "I'm proud of you" are music to a new mom's ears.

HOW IS DAD?

In all the excitement of bringing your baby home, supporting your partner in her recovery, and possibly returning to work, it's normal for dads to feel a little neglected. A 2021 study published in the *Journal of Affective Disorders* found that one in ten dads of infants displays symptoms of mental health disorders. So if you find yourself feeling not quite yourself, you're not alone.

That same study also uncovered one big risk factor for mental health disorder symptoms: lack of sleep. The authors wanted to know whether dad's answer to one question - "How are you sleeping?" - could predict symptoms of depression, anxiety, and other conditions. The result? Dads who responded to this question negatively had a much higher chance of mental health disorder symptoms.

I'm not bringing this up to alarm you or make you feel like doomsday is near. Lack of sleep isn't inevitable, and for some dads, the first month of their newborn's life is relaxing and not stressful. But for many, it's a challenging time, and that's okay. The most important thing is to communicate with your partner and let her know how you're feeling. Or reach out to a family member, friend, or medical professional to help you get through this time.

If you're like most parents you'll spend a lot of time oohing and aahing over your newborn during this first month. Newborns are almost like totally different kinds of creatures. It's crazy to think we all started out this way!

CHAPTER 5
GETTING THE HANG OF IT

 "I cannot think of any need in childhood as strong as the need for a father's protection." – Sigmund Freud

Your Baby's Milestones: Months 2 and 3			
Eating	Sleeping	Motor Skills	Language
Eats 4-6 ounces per feeding Goes through a growth spurt Might start cluster feeding	Sleeps an average of 14-17 hours per day Sleeps on his or her back Might go through a sleep regression	Still has newborn reflexes such as startle, rooting, stepping, and grasping reflex Shows neck control, might start to roll from back to side Tracks objects with eyes	Responds to facial expressions Starts to smile Coos and vocalizes

MONTH 2

THE FIRST MONTH has already passed, and you're starting to get the hang of things - and so is your baby. You'll probably notice your little one coming out of his shell a little this month. Here's what to expect during month two of your baby's life.

Feeding

I remember when our third baby was about six weeks old. My partner was at her limit with breastfeeding. "I just don't get it," she would say. "Just a few days ago, he was pretty much sleeping through the night, and now he wants to nurse every thirty minutes!"

At that moment, a light bulb went off. I remembered that our other two kids had done the *exact same thing*.

"Didn't this happen last time?" I asked.

After reviewing our mutual accounts of past history, we realized that yes, this had happened last time. And also the time before that. This caused us to do some additional research, and all sources ended up pointing to the same thing:

Cluster feeding. It might sound scary, but it's not. Or at least it's not *too* scary.

Cluster feeding happens when babies are going through a growth spurt. Basically, their little bodies say, "I want to eat ALL THE TIME." But fortunately, they can only keep that up for a few hours.

The solution for breastfeeding moms is to nurse on demand for a few hours while the baby is hungry so you all can get some well-earned sleep once the cluster-feeding session is done.

The good news is, if you can survive the nursing marathon, the baby will often get a deep snooze at the end. And that means you and mom can, too.

My number one recommendation? Find a Netflix show you both like and are willing to binge-watch while mom nurses the baby. I'm actually not joking. Passing the time in a fun way is key to success.

Sleeping

Your baby might be sleeping longer stretches at night, especially if she is cluster feeding right before falling asleep at night. Then again, she might not - it really varies.

You'll probably have a lot of people asking if your baby is sleeping through the night. Don't get discouraged if she's only sleeping a 4 or 5 hour stretch. At this age, that is considered "sleeping through the night" by doctors and child development experts! Generally speaking, over a 24-hour period, you should expect your baby to sleep 14 to 17 hours.

If you're still on paternity leave, don't forget what I told you last month: sleep when the baby sleeps whenever possible!

Bonding With Baby

Bonding with your baby this month is all about eye contact and communication. Newborns are pretty easygoing during the first month - they kind of just eat, sleep, and poop. In the second month, they begin to look around, verbalize, and respond to their environment a lot more (as described in the next section).

This month, bond with your baby by talking to him and making faces at each other. It sounds ridiculous, but it's actually pretty addicting when you see your little guy responding!

Tummy time is also a great opportunity for bonding time, and the 2-month mark is a great time to start since your baby is probably showing a lot more neck control. Schedule a daily bonding session/tummy time - it will help your baby's development while also giving you guys time to get to know each other.

At this early age, tummy time is pretty simple:

1. Place the baby on his tummy on your chest, ideally skin-to-skin.
2. Talk to your baby and smile at him while he attempts to lift his head and look in your eyes. It takes a lot of effort!

Tummy time can be exhausting for your little guy, so start with a few minutes and work up from there. He'll build a bit more strength each month with your help!

Learning

You might have noticed your baby is a little more interactive this month. It's very normal for babies this age to begin vocalizing (i.e., cooing or making other cute baby noises aside from the initial crying and grunting sounds).

Your baby's senses have made leaps and bounds in the last month. This month, he will become much more responsive to noise, light, and motion. It's a pretty amazing process to watch!

Eye contact is also a huge factor in baby's brain development. Here's what researchers have to say about what babies can gain just by looking into their caregiver's eyes:

"Babies who gaze into their parents' eyes also receive key social cues that help to speed the next stage of language learning—the understanding of the meaning of actual words. Andrew Meltzoff of the University of Washington has shown that young children who follow the direction of an adult's gaze pick up more vocabulary in the first two years of life than children who do not track these eye movements." (Kuhl, 2015)

Here are a few other exciting learning moments to look out for this month:

1. **Recognizing facial expressions:** You might notice your baby responding to your facial expressions this month. For example, if you make a dramatic samurai face, your baby might raise his eyebrows or - if you're lucky - coo in delight. Pretty great!
2. **Tracking objects:** Newborns aren't very good at watching individual objects. This month, your baby will start to be able to follow slow-moving objects with his eyes.
3. **Sending clearer messages:** Your baby will start to communicate a little bit better this month, now that he's starting to use his hands more. For example, he might start bringing his hands to his mouth when he's hungry or wants a pacifier.

Reading your baby's signs is one of the most exciting things about being a dad. There's something really amazing about being able to tap into your child's needs and meet them faster and better. But of course, it takes some trial and error.

My advice is not to miss out on these very early moments of communication. You'll remember them forever. I still make fun of our oldest because the only way she would be calmed as a newborn was if I blared reggae music and walked around our house holding her in the football position. I'm still pretty proud of those dad skills.

Keeping Baby Safe

Not much new is happening in the way of childproofing this month. Two-month-old babies are still relatively immobile. However, your baby is probably moving around a lot more, so stay vigilant about creating a clear sleeping space. Remember, months 2-4 are the riskiest when it comes to SIDS, so safe sleep is crucial.

How is Mom?

Now that your partner may be feeling more mobile, you might be tempted to back off on offering to help. But this is one of the best times to offer some additional help so she can take an occasional break.

Ask if she wants you to hold the baby at a certain time each day while she goes for a walk. Or better yet, if your baby takes a bottle, volunteer to take over one feeding so mom can have a little alone time. Having a little alone time - even if it's just ten minutes - can give her the opportunity to relax, reflect, and recover from childbirth.

A quick note: If other people have offered help and your partner has turned them down, don't assume she would respond the same way if you made the offer. It's normal for new moms to be on the protective side, but you have already earned her trust by being with her through pregnancy, delivery, and the first month. So don't be afraid to offer help, even if she doesn't seem willing to take it from others!

How is Dad?

If you're like the average dad in America, you've probably been back at work for a while now. (The average paternity leave in the U.S. is only one week.) And if you're like me, you might be struggling with that.

After my first daughter was born, I was back at work after eight days. Since my partner had a c-section, her recovery took a bit longer. I tried to be supportive and positive, but honestly, I was pretty frustrated about returning to work so soon. All I really wanted to do was hang out with my partner and new baby daughter. At the same time, I was totally exhausted by the time I got home from work, so I felt a little worthless in terms of help with cleaning and helping my partner.

We got through it, but it was hard. But years later, I learned about something I wish I had known at the time: postpartum doulas.

A postpartum doula comes to your home to help with newborn care. Overnight postpartum doulas come at night to take care of the baby so you and your partner can sleep. She or he will also complete basic household tasks, like dishes, laundry, or organizing baby clothes…all while you sleep.

How had I never heard of this before?

If you're struggling with the postpartum period, I highly recommend looking into postpartum doula support. They can be a bit pricey, but it's totally worth it. Doulas in training will also often work at a lower hourly rate, so if you're on a budget, consider hiring a doula in training.

The second month definitely has its ups and downs. Everyone is adjusting rapidly and it might seem overwhelming at times. Lean on your partner for support - she understands better than anyone else what it's like!

MONTH 3

Think about this: just 90 days ago, you hadn't met your baby. Now he's smiling, cooing, and starting to get mobile. Month three might be my favorite month of a baby's first year. Here are some things to look out for.

Feeding

Your baby's stomach has grown rapidly over the last three months. When your baby was three days old, her stomach's capacity was one ounce, max. At three months, her stomach can hold six ounces at a time. That's a pretty dramatic increase!

Three months is also typically a growth spurt period, which means your baby might need to eat more than usual. So if you notice she's taking more formula or breastfeeding a lot more than usual, you're not crazy!

Growth spurts are a regular occurrence in your baby's first year of life. Here are some signs that indicate your baby might be going through one:

- Increase in fussiness
- More frequent waking at night
- And of course, more eating!

It can be tough to get through growth spurts, and if your partner is exclusively breastfeeding, it can be especially challenging for her. Just remember - this too will pass! Thankfully, growth spurt periods usually only last a few days. And once this one is over, most babies don't have another one until the six-month mark.

Sleeping

A lot of parents start thinking about sleep schedules for their babies around this time. There's definitely nothing wrong with starting to work towards a schedule, but just remember that there are still a lot of changes going on, so you'll want to be flexible.

In fact, you might want to hold off on sleep training altogether at this point, since three months is a classic time for babies to go through a sleep regression. What does that mean? Let's say your baby has been sleeping for five-hour stretches for the last month. All of a sudden, he's awake every two hours. Not only that, but he doesn't seem to nap as much during the day. This is a classic case of sleep regression, and it's very common for it to happen right around three months of age.

So why is this happening? For one thing, as noted above, your baby is probably going through a growth spurt. It's normal for sleep regressions to occur alongside growth spurts.

But there's another reason: your baby's sleep cycle is changing. Specifically, your baby is developing what we adults know as "circadian rhythm."

Circadian rhythm is basically a fancy way of describing the human body's 24-hour cycle. (Fun fact: the word "circadian" comes from the Latin "circa diem," which means "around a day.") When your circadian rhythm is thrown off, it can cause all kinds of problems, from digestive issues to depression.

It takes about two months for your baby's circadian rhythm to develop. When you hear people talk about newborns "having their days and nights mixed up," they're kind of correct - except that newborns don't really have a sense of day and night at all! Around the third month, your baby will transition to a more dependable sleep/wake cycle. Although baby sleep needs are different from adult sleep needs, you'll notice that he tends to be more awake during the day and sleeps more at night.

But before that magical moment, there is a transition period - and transitions can be challenging. The 3- or 4-month sleep regression so many parents know is a mark that this transition is happening. Your baby's chemistry is going through a huge change, and it can cause things to seem like they're getting worse.

But it's also the case that things will get better. Just when you've thought you can't take one more night of this, your baby will suddenly sleep a five-hour stretch. Hang in there! This too will pass.

Bonding With Baby

Who doesn't like a good massage? This month, take some time to learn basic baby massage techniques. Baby massage has been shown to reduce colic, improve sleep, and aid in growth and development. Here are a few simple baby massage tips to try this month:

- Gently massage baby's feet as she is falling asleep
- Place baby on her tummy and gently rub her lower back
- Wear baby in a newborn wrap and gently massage her back and feet while walking

Some experts recommend using a baby oil when you massage your baby, but it's not totally necessary. If your baby is extremely awake or active, wait a while before trying massage. You want to choose a time when baby is relaxed and ready to fall asleep!

Not only does infant massage help with common newborn challenges, but some studies also suggest it helps with father-baby bonding. It's a win-win!

Learning

We talked about the bonding benefits of tummy time last month, but I didn't really touch on some of the developmental advantages of regular tummy time. Science has studied this pretty thoroughly, so there's quite a bit of evidence out there!

Here are some of the ways tummy time has been proven to benefit your baby, as concluded by a 2020 study of over 4,200 participants:

- Prevents brachycephaly (a condition that results in a flattened head and requires treatment)
- Improves gross motor skill development
- Reduces body mass index/BMI
- Improves ease of crawling and rolling

So keep up your daily tummy time sessions - they're not only great for bonding but also for your baby's development!

Keeping Baby Safe

This month you might notice your baby starting to roll from his back to his side. This is the beginning of a new parenting stage: trying to keep up with your baby's ever-increasing mobility.

For now, the biggest childproofing item to keep in mind is preventing your baby from taking a fall. For example, up to this point, you may have occasionally set the baby down in the middle of your bed or on a sofa. Not anymore. All those signs on the diaper changing tables about not leaving the baby unattended are about to get real. You would be surprised how quickly a baby this small can move!

Always keep a hand on the baby on a high surface, and make sure the crib rails are correctly installed. The risk of SIDS and suffocation is still very real at this age, so even though it might be really tempting to put some of the baby's favorite toys and stuffed animals in the crib, hold off. It's not worth the risk!

Keep in mind that like any milestone, rolling doesn't *have* to happen this month. In fact, a lot of babies don't start rolling to their side for another month or two. But regardless, you'll be ready when it happens!

• • •

How is Mom?

It's been three months since your partner gave birth, and you might assume things are totally back to normal "down there" for her. But if she's like 35 percent of new moms, she might be dealing with urinary incontinence. Or if she's like 20 percent of women who have given birth for the first time, she may have severe pelvic floor injury that would greatly benefit from treatment.

You would think new dads would hear more about this, but sadly, most dads I know are totally unfamiliar with these very common issues women face. Regardless of what type of delivery, birth is really hard on a woman's pelvic floor. It's important for your partner to know these issues are normal and that there are things she can do to recover and regain control.

Here are a few red flags to look out for. If you hear your partner mention any of these issues, encourage her to see her doctor. It's early enough that she can prevent a lot of problems down the road!

- Pain or a feeling of "bulging" in the pelvic area
- Loss of urinary control
- Loss of control of passing gas / feces
- Pain during and after intercourse

And speaking of intercourse, if she still isn't ready, be patient - especially if the birth was complicated or if she had stitches. Estrogen levels - which contribute to arousal - also drop significantly in the first months postpartum, even more so if your partner is exclusively breastfeeding. Encourage your partner to discuss any concerns with her physician to make sure there aren't any more serious and treatable problems.

How is Dad?

Postpartum depression (PPD) happens to dads, too. A 2019 study found that fathers were most likely to experience PPD between three and six months after the baby's birth. The researchers analyzed over 20,000 subjects and concluded that postpartum depression in new dads is "relatively common." Keep in mind that although dads are more likely to experience PPD if their partner is going through the same thing, this isn't always the case.

Here are some of the most common manifestations of PPD in dads:

- Irritability
- Extreme mood swings
- Indecisiveness
- Depressed mood and a feeling of hopelessness
- Insomnia
- Weight loss/gain or changes in appetite
- Loss of focus
- Suicidal thoughts
- Social withdrawal

If you experience these symptoms, be sure to speak with your doctor and seek help. Although PPD can resolve on its own, it tends to be a sort of landslide condition - if you ignore it too long, it can get much worse very quickly. Keep in mind that you are more likely to experience PPD if you have had depression before, if the pregnancy was unintended, if mom is suffering from depression, or if there are relationship difficulties.

Between growth spurts, feeding challenges, and your partner's recovery, the third month is quite a hurdle. Congratulations on getting through! The next months will bring better sleep, more cute baby moments, and increased confidence in your role as dad and partner.

CHAPTER 6
NEWBORN TO INFANT

"Son, brother, father, lover, friend. There is room in the heart for all the affections, as there is room in heaven for all the stars." —Victor Hugo

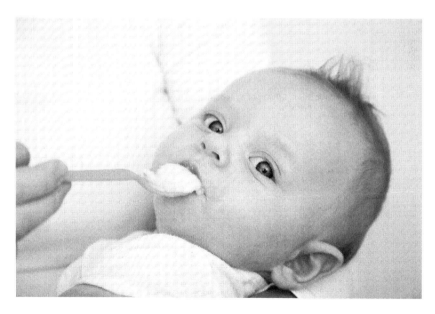

Your Baby's Milestones: Months 4 and 5			
Eating	**Sleeping**	**Motor Skills**	**Language**
Might show signs of solid food readiness Still needs around 24 ounces of milk per day	Sleeps about 15 hours per day Might be ready to start sleep training Discontinue use of inclined sleepers	Starts to put objects in mouth Starts to hold head steady - might sit with support	Plays peekaboo! Might start to laugh

MONTH 4

I HATE to break it to you, but your little baby is no longer a newborn. As of month four, he or she has been upgraded to the next level: infant.

The good news is, infancy is full of really great milestones. A few things to look forward to: solid food, non-gas-induced smiles, laughter, and more mobility. Here's what to expect in month four.

Feeding Baby

A quick Internet search reveals that there's a lot of debate out there as to when is the best time to introduce solid foods. My personal opinion (which has changed through the years as we've had more kids): Rule #1 is to *watch your baby*. If you see any of the following signs, it might indicate your baby is ready to start eating solid foods:

1. Your baby can hold his head up and sit with little or no support. (This one is a prerequisite, so don't move on if your baby doesn't have this down.)
2. Your baby doesn't have any feeding issues and can swallow easily.
3. Your baby gets frustrated and antsy when you and your partner eat. He might fuss or even grab at your food (be careful! He's more agile than he seems!). It's almost like he wants what you have. Chances are, he does, and it's time to show him the ropes.

Here are my top three starter foods to feed your baby if you decide to start solids this month:

Oatmeal: Oatmeal is my favorite first solid food. It's a great source of fiber, magnesium, and iron and is easy to prepare. Mix it with breast milk or formula. When the baby starts eating other fruit purees, I like to mix it in with oatmeal for the added fiber content.

Rice cereal: This is the classic first baby food for a reason. It's easy to feed your baby and is also relatively flavorless, so if you mix it with breastmilk or formula your baby is likely to enjoy it.

Avocado: Avocado is rich in healthy fats which have been shown to aid in your baby's brain development. Plus, it's just about the easiest first food out there. Simply slice a ripe avocado in half, scoop out a few tablespoons, and mash it up. Mix it with some breast milk or formula until it has a cereal-like consistency, then spoon-feed it to your baby.

Aside from breastmilk or formula, you don't need to add anything else to these foods, such as sugar or salt. Keep it simple!

Here are some instructions for successful baby feeding:

1. Prep your space. Have a damp washcloth or some paper towels on hand, as well as a baby bib.
2. Get baby ready. If it's warm enough, just take the baby's clothes off, down to the diaper. Easier cleanup that way!
3. Secure the bib around the baby's neck.
4. Get ready for his first bites! Make sure he opens his mouth to receive the food. You can lightly place the spoon on his bottom lip to encourage him to "Say ah!"
5. Feed the baby with a small baby spoon. It's totally normal for it to take a while for your baby to learn how to swallow food, so don't worry if he spits most of it up. At this point, there's no rush, and the amount of food your baby eats isn't important, since breastmilk or formula is the primary source of nutrition at this age.

It's also normal for feeding time to be messy, so be prepared to do some cleanup! I like to have a warm washcloth ready so I can give the baby and high chair a good wipe-down right away. No one likes cleaning up dried baby food!

Sleeping

You might have heard that your baby will sleep through the night once you start feeding solids. As much as I wish this were the case, research is still up in the air.

However, there was a promising study of over 1,303 babies in the U.K in 2018 that suggests early introduction of solids might actually help your baby (and you) sleep better. In the study, some of the babies were introduced to solid foods at four months, and others at six (the recommended age in the U.K.)

This is a summary of their findings:

"In a randomized clinical trial, the early introduction of solids into the infant's diet was associated with longer sleep duration, less frequent waking at night, and a reduction in reported very serious sleep problems."

Yes, you read that right - not only did introducing solids at four months help baby sleep longer and better, but it also correlated with fewer "very serious sleep problems" in caregivers. Sounds like a win-win!

However, keep in mind that if your baby isn't ready for solids, you probably won't see these benefits. In fact, it could backfire. So always go back to rule #1: watch your baby, and act accordingly.

Bonding With Baby

If you feel like you've got diapers, swaddling, and holding your baby mastered, it's time to consider another great dad bonding trick: baby wearing.

Baby wearing is exactly what it sounds like: attaching your baby to your body via a baby carrier and "wearing" him or her around the house, neighborhood, or wherever you happen to be.

When I first became a dad, baby wearing was just gaining popularity - with moms. Not dads. Now it's totally mainstream and normal to see dads toting their little tykes in a Baby Bjorn. I like to joke with my younger siblings and tell them I was the OG Baby wearing Dad.

In all seriousness, though, baby wearing is great for two primary reasons:

1. It encourages bonding
2. It can be really convenient

The second reason is only true if your baby likes being in a baby carrier. If your baby does not like being swaddled, he or she might not like being worn in a carrier. But it's still worth a shot!

Keep in mind that most standard baby carriers require a newborn insert for babies less than seven pounds. Wrap-style carriers are ideal at this stage, but personally, I found them challenging to use. Buckle-style carriers are much easier to take off and put on. They also offer great support for both the baby and the caregiver.

Here are some pro tips for successful baby wearing that won't be a pain in your neck (literally).

1. Make sure you keep your baby snug against your chest. I often see people wearing babies on the lower third of their torso - this is incorrect and could result in serious back pain. Also, it's less ideal for your baby since her head is less stable in this position. Don't let the baby hang off your torso. She should be snuggled in close and supported.
2. Keep the baby's legs in a frog or M-shape position, with the knees bent.
3. Don't wear your baby facing out just yet - her hips and legs are still developing, and this could put too much stress on her muscles.
4. Never wear your baby while you are cooking or doing other potentially hazardous activities.

It can be a bit tricky to get your baby comfy in the carrier the first few times, so make sure you have a helper nearby to assist if needed.

Not only is baby wearing great for a baby's feeling of security and comfort, but science suggests it's also beneficial for caregivers. For example, in a recent study, researchers investigated the effects of baby wearing on parents whose babies had a NICU stay. They found that baby wearing reduced parental feelings of stress and anxiety and increased feelings of parental empowerment. Pretty amazing!

Learning

This month, it's time for your baby's four-month checkup! The pediatrician will be checking the following:

- Weight, height, head circumference measurements
- Physical exam - check for reflexes, color, muscle tone
- Updated vaccines - your baby will probably receive round 2 of the recommended vaccines for this age. These are typically DTap, polio, and Hib.

The doctor might also ask if your baby is sitting with support yet. Although this usually starts around four or five months, don't stress if your baby isn't quite there. Head control should be slowly stabilizing at this point, however.

Before your baby's checkup, take some time to sit down and write out any questions you might have for your pediatrician. I can't tell you how many times my partner and I have responded with a deer-in-the-headlights look when the doctor asks if we have any questions, only to remember a whole list a few hours later!

Keeping Baby Safe

Now that your baby is able to put things in his or her mouth, it's time to do a quick check around the house for chokeable items.

Small objects under 1.5 inches in diameter are among the most common choking causes at this age. These might include buttons, bottle caps, coins, Legos, cough drops, peanuts and chewable vitamins. It might seem unlikely that your baby would encounter one of these items, but it's amazing how many small objects wind up on the floor or in baby's reach.

One team of researchers recommends the following test for whether or not an item is a choking hazard. Take a toilet paper roll and see if the object passes through it without any resistance. If so, the item is considered chokeable.

And of course, make sure to never give your baby any foods that could cause choking. Hot dogs, peanuts, popcorn, and grapes are some of the leading culprits.

How is Mom?

At this point, your partner may be feeling ready to get back to exercise - even if that just looks like a walk around the block. But there's something you both should be aware of before she resumes exercise: diastasis recti, or separation of the abdominal muscles.

Diastasis recti is a separation of the muscle called rectus abdominis - in laymen's terms, the six-pack muscles. This condition is extremely common after pregnancy and affects 60 percent of women who have had children. It usually resolves on its own after eight weeks, but 40 percent of women will still experience symptoms after that point.

Diastasis recti results from the high amount of pressure the growing uterus places on the abdominal muscles. During pregnancy, the layer of tissue between the six-pack muscles stretches and thins out. Sometimes, it becomes stretched a bit too much, resulting in diastasis recti. This usually happens in the third trimester.

If your partner experiences any of the following symptoms on a regular basis, she should be assessed for diastasis recti:

- A bulging in the abdomen, just above the bellybutton
- Difficulty lifting objects
- Pelvic pain
- Incontinence
- A feeling of weakness in the abdominal region
- Heartburn and indigestion
- Pain during intercourse

You might notice these symptoms are similar to the ones we discussed in chapter five. That's because the pelvic floor and core musculature work together. Core stability problems often go hand-in-hand with pelvic floor problems, and vice versa. And when you think about the changes your partner's body has gone through in the last year, it makes sense that childbirth often contributes to these issues.

Women with diastasis recti should avoid the following exercises:

- Crunches/sit-ups
- Plank
- Pilates core exercises
- Burpees
- Mountain climbers

Basically, she should avoid any exercises that put pressure on the abdominal region. Exercises like plank use gravity to strengthen the core - which is why they are great core exercises! But only if your abdominal muscles aren't separated.

The good news is, diastasis recti usually resolves without a lot of intervention. If your partner's abdominal separation is severe, she would probably benefit from physical therapy. My partner had diastasis recti after our second child was born. Although it was definitely not pleasant, with patience it resolved after about six months. This was eleven years ago, and it was difficult at that time to find someone to help her with it. Fortunately, awareness surrounding diastasis recti has greatly increased since then.

Encourage your partner to discuss diastasis recti with her healthcare provider and get an assessment, especially if she is planning to resume exercise soon. Although it's not an extremely dangerous condition, unresolved diastasis recti can lead to long-term problems like pelvic floor disorders and back pain.

How is Dad?

Most women return to work around this time, so you might be feeling a little added pressure if that's the case. Make sure to take time to do something you enjoy, be it a hobby, physical activity, or just watching your favorite sport and some friends.

If your baby care responsibilities have increased because your partner is back at work (or for any reason!), try to brainstorm ways to have fun while taking care of the baby. For example, I'm a pretty social person by nature and enjoy getting together with friends. After our babies were born and my partner started working again, I would have a few friends over on the weekend to watch soccer. This worked out well because I could easily supervise the baby while also hanging out with friends.

I always feel like the end of month four is kind of like coming out of a tunnel. Life is getting back to normal, and your baby is becoming less mysterious every day. It's amazing to see their little personalities slowly emerge!

MONTH 5

By month five, your baby is feeling less like a fragile doll and more like a chunky little human. At this point, most babies have more than doubled their birth weight. Think about that for a minute: can you imagine doubling your body weight over the course of a five-month period? Probably not a very pretty mental picture!

This month your baby will continue to pack on the pounds, and will become a lot chattier. This is also a good time to start thinking about sleep training.

Feeding

You might notice your baby is feeding less frequently as you move into the fifth month. Your baby's stomach has grown a lot, so she's able to take in more milk at feedings. This also translates into fewer diaper changes!

Keep watching your baby for signs she is ready to start solids. If you've already gotten a start in month four, you can add on to your baby's food choices this month.

Here is a list of some great starter foods to feed your baby in month five, assuming she has already started eating solids. If not, go back to month four and start with those suggestions.

My Top 3 Fruits for 5 Months:

- Apples: Babies love applesauce. Apples are high in vitamin C which helps your baby's immune system.
- Bananas: Bananas are easy to prepare on your own, and also available as ready-made purees. Bananas can be constipating, so I like to pair them with oatmeal which provides fiber to help ease your baby's digestion.
- Pears: Pears have a slightly sweet flavor and are also high in fiber.

My Top 3 Vegetables for 5 Months:

- Sweet potatoes: Sweet potatoes are always our babies' favorites. They're also a great source of carbohydrates for healthy energy and easy to prepare at home.

- Green beans: I'm always surprised at how much our babies enjoy pureed green beans. This classic baby food is packed with vitamins A, B, and C.
- Carrots: Carrots are an excellent source of vitamin A, and their slight sweetness makes them a baby's delight.

As you can see, this month, we are adding some fruits and veggies into the mix. These are great sources of dietary fiber (which is important because it prevents constipation), as well as micronutrients like vitamin C, vitamin A, and the B vitamins. They're also easy to mix with foods your baby is already eating to make the adjustment easier.

Be sure to wait a few days after you give the baby new food. For example, if you introduce bananas on a Monday, wait until Wednesday to offer sweet potatoes. This gives the baby a chance to get used to the new foods and also allows you to observe whether or not the food settles well with her. Remember, breast milk or formula is still the only food your baby really needs at this point, so if she doesn't seem very excited about solid foods, don't fret.

If you observe any of the following signs after introducing a new food, discontinue feeding it until your baby is a bit older and consult with your doctor:

- Hives or rash
- Vomiting
- Swelling of the lips
- Wheezing or unusual sneezing

Seek medical help immediately if the baby has trouble breathing or swallowing.

Sleeping

Now that your baby's sleep has become more regulated, it's time to start thinking about sleep training. There are so many sleep training methods out there, but in my experience, they really boil down to two big categories:

1. **Cry It Out:** For this method, you basically put your baby down at the desired bedtime and allow him to cry himself to sleep, or "cry it out." Proponents of this method note that while it can be hard the first few nights, eventually your baby will sleep through the night earlier and more successfully if you stick with it.
2. **Check and Console:** This method is similar, except instead of leaving the baby, you go in and make visits at regular intervals. Each night you gradually decrease the number of visits. My partner and I have used this method successfully with our children, and they are all great sleepers!

So what approach is best? It really depends. I would recommend researching different methods and choosing the one that clicks best with your personality and lifestyle. There are some great books in the References section that go in-depth on this topic.

Regardless of the method you choose, make sure it's right *for you*. You'll hear a lot of people throwing opinions around about sleep training, but ultimately the best approach is one that works best for you, your partner, and your baby.

Bonding With Baby

Establishing rituals goes hand-in-hand with sleep training, but I've put this in the bonding section because I believe it's something parents might take for granted. This month is a great time to start to develop routines with your baby. Not only will routines make big life changes like sleep training and going back to work easier on the baby (and you and your partner!), but they also encourage better bonding for a simple reason: babies who have routines and rituals feel secure and develop trust for their caregivers.

Think about it for a minute. Let's imagine you have a caregiver who's very nice but who has no structure in their daily routine. Every day is a new adventure and you never know what to expect. This sounds exciting, but it's just overwhelming for a tiny human being trying to adjust to life in the world.

Now let's take the same nice caregiver and add in routine. Every day at a certain time, the baby is fed, bathed, or put down for a nap. The baby quickly learns not only what the routine is, but also *who* the person associated with the routine is. Therefore, the baby learns to trust not just the schedule but the people responsible for it - you and your partner.

This month, try adding one routine into your baby's - and your - day. It could be something as simple as going for a 10-minute walk at the same time every day, or giving baby a bath just before putting on his pajamas. Not only will this help your baby feel secure, but it will also create a great space for bonding and togetherness.

Learning

I remember when my first child was born, I was very disappointed at how long it took her to figure out peek-a-boo. If you're in the same boat, I have great news. Your baby's sense of object permanence is pretty much worked out at this point, so there's lots of peek-a-boo in store for you.

Around the age of five months, babies figure out that just because something disappears from view doesn't mean it's gone. It might seem like a small thing, but this is a huge jump in brain development. And since your baby is also starting to smile and laugh, month five has some pretty fun moments.

Keeping Baby Safe

Your baby can probably roll at this point, so it's important to stop using any incline sleepers. Incline sleepers became incredibly popular, and for good reason - they are amazing at helping babies sleep, since they situate the baby in an upright position. This helps especially with issues like GERD.

Unfortunately, incline sleepers have decreased in popularity just as fast. In 2019 Fisher Price recalled the Rock 'n' Play after over 30 infant deaths related to the product were reported, which shocked the parenting world. The Rock 'n' Play had been the gold standard of baby sleepers for about a decade, up until this point.

Incline sleepers are especially dangerous once the baby starts rolling. If you have one and have been using it up to this point, don't panic, but be aware that most pediatricians do not recommend using them for sleep. We have an old Rock 'n' Play that we received as a gift before the recall, and still use ours to put the baby in from time to time if we're nearby and the baby is in our sight. But the Rock 'n' Play or any incline sleeper should never be used as a sleeping space. The danger of entrapment has been shown to be high, especially for babies who are able to roll.

How is Mom?

If your partner is going back to work this month, she may be feeling overwhelmed, sad, or even guilty. Be sure to check in with her frequently and give her positive moral support. Reassure her that she's doing a great job.

Here are five simple things you can do to support your partner when she returns to work:

1. Take over dinner for a few nights of the week if you haven't already. That might mean cooking, or it might mean ordering takeout.

2. Arrange for a surprise date night. Ask a close friend or family member, or a babysitter you trust, to watch the baby for a few hours while you take your partner out for some R&R.

3. Take over some cleaning tasks, or hire someone temporarily to help out with cleaning the house. This way, your partner can come home and focus on spending time with you and the baby instead of cleaning.

4. Visit her at work on her lunch break with the baby, or any time it's possible. Or if that's not possible, send her photos if you're home with the baby.

5. Give her a lot of support if she is pumping. She might feel anxious about not providing enough milk or even struggle to pump at first. Ask how you can help her make the process as simple as possible.

Remember that the return to work is a big adjustment, and it might take a few weeks for everyone to get in the groove. Remind your partner often that you are there for her and the baby - just hearing this reassurance means a lot!

If you are planning to put your baby in daycare or hire a nanny, make sure you allow plenty of time to find a caregiver you really trust. I remember when my partner went back to work after our third child was born, and she wasn't totally happy with our childcare situation. After a few weeks, she seemed really down, so I asked a trusted family member who had offered help if she could take over just for a couple of days. It was amazing to see how much this relieved stress for my partner and made me realize how critical it is that you have the right care provider.

How is Dad?

Remember when we were talking about object permanence and how fun it is now that your baby can recognize objects aren't gone when they disappear from sight? Well, there's also a downside to your baby's newfound sense of permanence: she now knows when her parent leaves the room, and chances are she isn't very happy about it.

Gone are the days when you could simply hand your baby off to unfamiliar people at dinner parties and family get-togethers. Separation anxiety is very common at this age, and it can make life difficult.

Additionally, I remember being discouraged at this stage because our babies only wanted mom. Don't take it personally! Your baby is still attached to you, but it's common for babies to cling to mom at this age, especially if they are exclusively breastfed. Try not to get offended or interpret this as the baby not feeling secure with you.

Like all parenting challenges, separation anxiety fades away with time and it gets easier! For now, keep in mind that this is a normal stage and simply means your baby is growing up.

Between peek-a-boo, solid foods, and more consistent sleep, month five marks a huge jump in your baby's development. Before you know it, he'll be scooting around the house and getting in all kinds of trouble. Enjoy this stage while it lasts!

CHAPTER 7
HALF WAY THERE

 "In my career, there's many things I've won and many things I've achieved, but for me, my greatest achievement is my children and my family." —David Beckham

Your Baby's Milestones: Months 6 and 7			
Eating	**Sleeping**	**Motor Skills**	**Language**
Eats about 25 ounces per day Takes 8 ounces per feeding 6-month growth spurt	Sleeps an average of 14-15 hours per day Takes 3 naps per day	Starts to scoot/crawl Enjoys board books	Responds to sounds/baby talk Takes turns imitating sounds

MONTH 6

YOU'RE HALFWAY through your baby's first year! It might feel like your son or daughter has been around forever, or it might feel like only yesterday he or she was born. Chances are, it's a mix of both.

Your baby will go through a lot of big changes this month, and his or her personality will really blossom. Get ready for a fun month ahead!

Feeding

Typically a 6-month-old needs approximately six 6-8 oz formula feedings per day or about 25 ounces of breastmilk.

If your partner is breastfeeding, she might feel a little more at ease about nursing frequency for most of the month. But chances are, at some point, she will also feel like the baby is nursing more this month than last. That would make sense because most babies go through another big growth spurt right around the six-month mark!

If you forgot about growth spurts, go back to chapter five, where I discussed the common 3-month growth spurt most babies experience. The 6-month growth spurt will be more of the same!

If your baby is going through a growth spurt, he might go back to nursing every two or three hours. But once he's through the rapid growth period, things should calm down. Babies usually only need to nurse every three or four hours once they hit the six-month mark.

Your baby might seem extra fussy this month, and you might think it's food-related, but consider this: many babies start cutting teeth around the age of six months. If your baby seems frustrated and you know he has been eating and sleeping enough, you're probably dealing with incoming chompers.

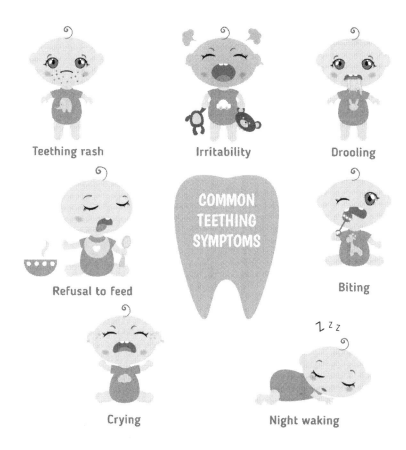

Teething rash

Irritability

Drooling

COMMON TEETHING SYMPTOMS

Refusal to feed

Biting

Crying

Night waking

Here are a few common signs that your baby might be teething:

- Excessive drool
- Red gums
- Mild temperature (less than 100.4 degrees Fahrenheit)
- Pulling or rubbing ears
- Flushed cheeks
- Sleeplessness
- Fretfulness

Sounds like fun, right? Teething can be a challenging period for babies and parents, but there are a few things you can do to support your baby as he goes through this time. Try rubbing your baby's gums (with a clean finger, of course!) and letting him gnaw on your finger a bit. You can also purchase teething rings that you put in the fridge to cool. The cold offers babies a lot of relief from teething symptoms.

So what teeth emerge first? Watch the baby's bottom gums for the two middle teeth, which usually erupt around this time - or possibly later. The top two teeth will usually come in shortly after. However, each baby is different, so your little guy or gal might follow a different pattern. Likewise, it's hard to predict how babies will tolerate teething. Our third baby got all four of his first teeth in a week and barely even whimpered about it. Baby #5 took forever to cut her first tooth and was quite the drama queen. You never know!

Temporary Teeth Chart

Names / Groups		Eruption	Shedding
Central Incisor		8 - 12 mos.	6 - 7 yrs.
Lateral Incisor		9 - 13 mos.	7 - 8 yrs.
Canine		16 - 22 mos.	10 - 12 yrs.
First Molar		13 - 19 mos.	9 - 11 yrs.
Second Molar		25- 33 mos.	10- 12 yrs.
		23 - 31 mos.	10 - 12 yrs.
Molars		14 - 18 mos.	9 - 11 yrs.
Canine		17 - 23 mos.	9 - 12 yrs.
		10 - 16 mos.	7 - 8 yrs.
Incisors		6- 10 mos.	6- 7 yrs.

Sleeping

Around six months, my partner and I always have a rude awakening. Just when we've gotten used to the baby napping at least three times a day, suddenly the third nap just disappears. Poof! Into thin air.

Here's another common scenario: you *thought* he was sleeping through the night, but now this month, the joke's on you. He's waking every two or three hours for the first time since his first week home. Between the lack of naps and the frequent waking, you might like your baby has once again decided to fool you.

If you find yourself in a similar situation this month, rest assured that it's totally normal. Your baby is going through a lot of changes in his sixth month, from growth spurts to teething, so it makes sense that sleep patterns would get a little wonky. Your baby is probably also a lot more mobile now, so he may just be rolling around and waking himself up! Try to hang in there and remember: this is just a phase. It will pass.

Speaking of being more mobile, you might find that even though you put your baby to sleep on his back, he ends up on his stomach. You don't need to disturb him and flip him back over - if he's strong enough to flip from his stomach to his back, it's okay for him to sleep on his back. But for the time being, keep putting him down on his tummy to start out.

A final note on sleep this month: expect your baby to sleep about 14-15 total hours per day. Usually, that's about two naps per day totaling 3 or 4 hours, and 10 or 11 hours at night.

Bonding With Baby

Bonding is all about communication, and your baby is probably becoming quite the chatterbox. Encourage his verbal skills while also strengthening your bond by talking back to him when he talks to you. At this age, babies love to hear themselves talk, but they love it even more when someone responds in baby talk.

Try this: the next time your baby starts babbling, try imitating it back to her. This might seem ridiculous, but studies have shown that speaking "baby talk" to your baby actually helps her learn the ins and outs of human language and develops her verbal skills. Plus, it teaches her to trust you. All that babbling going on in the high chair is, to her, a human dialogue when you join in.

So grab a cup of coffee, have a seat at the table, and take some time to chat. I can't think of a better bonding activity for this age!

Learning

This month your baby has his or her six-month checkup! In addition to all the usual items, your pediatrician will probably ask you about common milestones your baby has reached or will reach soon. These include responding to sounds, taking turns making sounds with you or another caregiver, reaching for objects, recognizing themselves in a mirror, or making basic consonant sounds.

If your baby hasn't met all these milestones yet, don't fret - but do be sure to mention it to your doctor at the appointment.

You might have noticed your baby has learned a major motor skill this month, if not earlier: pushing up with his arms. This might seem like a small thing, but it's actually a huge step toward crawling. Once babies can roll and push up with confidence, you can expect some variation of crawling to be right around the corner. Get ready!

Keeping Baby Safe

I know it's hard to believe, but your baby is probably on the verge of crawling. You might as well save the stress and childproof everything now, so you can enjoy watching her learn to crawl when it happens (it's pretty entertaining!).

You can continue to work on this as your baby gets older, but for now, there are a few simple things to accomplish:

- Make sure all electric cords are inaccessible or at least out of sight (for example, behind heavy furniture your baby cannot reach).

- Keep any space heaters, radiators, or other hot surfaces out of reach - you can block them off with baby gates if need be.
- Cover all electric outlets.
- Continue to keep items your baby could choke on off the floor or any other area your baby can reach.

First and foremost, keep the baby in your sight. It's fine for her to sleep in a different room, but when she's awake, she should be somewhere she can see you. Your dad intuition is better able to kick in when you have her in sight.

How is Mom?

If your partner is exclusively breastfeeding and your baby is going through a growth spurt, remember the tips I shared from month three. Encourage your partner to try pumping one bottle each day so you can help with a feeding or two - ideally at night or whenever your partner could most use the sleep. Growth spurts are hard on everyone, but when mom is the sole source of nourishment, they can be especially challenging for her!

Many women notice that their milk supply seems to drop around the 6-month mark. If your partner is concerned about this, she should consult with her doctor or a lactation consultant. There are a lot of things she can try if she wants to boost her milk supply, but make sure she has the essentials covered: a healthy diet, good hydration, and adequate sleep.

How is Dad?

I'll admit: I used to think the advice to enjoy the moment was pretty cliche and trite. But after years of doing this dad thing, I've softened my opinion. This first year with your son or daughter is going to fly by, and you can't get the time back.

Take some time this month to just be with your baby. Don't worry about hitting milestones, sleep schedules, or fine and gross motor skills - just enjoy his or her presence. That could mean taking a walk in nature, having some quality tummy time, or watching your favorite show together. You're halfway through the first year of life - soak it in.

The six-month mark isn't without its challenges (like all things parenting!), but just take it one day at a time. Oh, and if you remember - take lots of pictures. This stage has some pretty cute moments, from smiles to laughs, to really messy food moments.

MONTH 7

Seven months in, you might be feeling a little anxious for your baby to be able to do more stuff. Rest assured, this month has a lot of fun in store. Before you know it, you'll be wishing your baby was a newborn again. I'm not going to lie: older babies can be a handful, but as I always say, it keeps you young.

Feeding

If your baby has been enjoying solid foods for the last few months, you can introduce a few new foods this month. Nutrient-packed vegetables like butternut squash, peas, and acorn squash are great options for purees, but you might also consider serving some of the baby's familiar foods as finger foods. For example, if your baby enjoyed avocados, you can serve them thinly sliced instead of mashed. Give it a shot and see how your baby responds!

Speaking of finger foods and baby feeding himself, you might have heard buzz about something called "baby-led weaning." This approach encourages parents to follow baby's lead when it comes to eating. At this age, that looks like putting a bunch of baby foods (prepared for safe eating, of course) on the highchair tray and letting baby go at it.

My partner learned about baby-led weaning when our first child was a baby, and we've been doing it ever since. Like any parenting philosophy, it has its pros and cons, but we've had an overwhelmingly positive experience. Here are just a few of the benefits we've seen firsthand in our own kids:

1. Leads to decreased pickiness. Our kids eat everything, and they've been that way since they started eating.
2. It's way more cost-effective. You don't have to worry about buying fancy baby food purees - just feed the baby simple foods you already eat.
3. Easier to control ingredients. I know exactly what my baby is eating. Given some of the questionable ingredients in commercially made baby food, that's really reassuring.
4. It's just easier. Personally, I find it much easier to dice up a banana in tiny pieces and put it on the baby's tray than it is to sit and spoon-feed.

The one big downside is that baby-led weaning is messy. Make sure you have a bib and some towels on hand for easy cleanup.

Sleeping

My partner was sick with mastitis (more on that below) around this time when our fourth child was a baby. She was so sick she couldn't keep up with the laundry, and I wasn't doing a great job supporting her in that regard, so at a certain point, she threw up her hands and told me to just buy the baby some new pajamas on the way home from work. That sounded like a good plan (less laundry is always good, right?), so I agreed it was the best idea.

But little did I know, the world of baby pajamas is more complicated than I realized! I had no idea there were so many options. As it turns out, finding the right pair of pajamas can be important if your little guy is picky about his pj's. Sadly, in my case, I brought home a 3-pack of footed pajamas, only to find out our son despises them and prefers a sleep sack. Lesson learned!

Here's a breakdown of three of the common types of baby pajamas:

Footed pajamas

These are the classic ones that have the feet attached. They are most commonly made with either zippers or snaps, although now there are even magnetic closure options!

Pros:

- These are convenient because you don't have to worry about your baby's feet getting cold.
- Footed pj's are also pretty simple when it comes to diaper changes.

Cons:

- Some babies don't like having their feet covered (case in point: my son).
- This sounds crazy, but there is a risk your baby could develop what's called a hair tourniquet, which is exactly what it sounds like: a piece of hair wrapped around your baby's toe that can cut off circulation. While footed pj's don't cause these, they can make it easier to miss them, so just be sure to check every so often!

Sleep Sacks

Sleep sacks are what they sound like: a big sack that your baby sleeps in. They usually close with a zipper. I like to use sleep sacks with a onesie underneath and a pair of baby socks (unless the baby doesn't like socks).

Pros:

- Sleep sacks give the baby a lot of room to move around, and allow you to decide whether or not to cover the baby's feet.
- The airflow helps the baby with temperature control at night.
- Some doctors recommend sleep sacks because parents are less likely to use blankets (which are still a safety hazard) when the baby is in a sleep sack.

Cons:

- Sleep sacks make diaper changes a little more complicated.
- Your baby might not like all the extra fabric.

Sleep Gowns

Sleep gowns are similar to sleep sacks, but instead of being closed in, the bottom is open and lined with elastic. They're super cute and usually long-sleeved, so you don't need any additional onesies, but a pair of socks might still be a good idea.

Pros:

- Sleep gowns make diaper changes very easy!
- Can be worn with or without socks.

Cons:

- Personally, I like sleep gowns for younger, less wiggly babies who aren't likely to move around and kick their legs out. This creates a lot of excess fabric at the top of the baby's torso, which isn't as safe (or comfortable!) as other options.

As with a lot of parenting topics, opinions abound as to what is the best type of pajama for babies. My opinion: the best option is the one your baby sleeps best in (provided that first and foremost, it's safe!). Understanding his or her sleep preferences will help everyone get more sleep - try to get to know them this month!

· · ·

Bonding With Baby

It might sound crazy, but talking to your baby is one of the best ways to deepen your bond - and this month, he might even start to babble right back at you!

Multiple studies have found that babies whose parents speak to them from infancy go on to develop verbal skills more easily and may even have fewer academic difficulties later in life.

And while I'm on the topic, let's discuss "baby talk" - you know, that high-pitched way of talking adults always take on when they're speaking to infants or toddlers. I'll admit that before I became a dad, I couldn't stand baby talk, and I swore I would never talk to my child that way.

Like other ideas, this one also changed. Every time I talked to my daughter, I found myself speaking six octaves higher than normal. I don't recall ever making the choice to change my mind - it just happened. But one thing was clear: *she* liked baby talk. And once she hit six or seven months, she would even talk back, which was pretty awesome.

Believe it or not, there have actually been studies done on the benefits of baby talk - or "parentese" as it is sometimes called. Here's one amazing finding from some of her research:

"Parentese exaggerates differences between sounds—one phoneme can be easily discriminated from another. Our studies show that exaggerated speech most likely helps infants as they commit these sounds to memory. In a recent study by my group, Nairán Ramírez-Esparza, now at the University of Connecticut, had infants wear high-fidelity miniature tape recorders fitted into lightweight vests worn at home throughout the day. The recordings let us enter the children's auditory world and showed that if their parents spoke to them in parentese at that age, then one year later these infants had learned more than twice the number of words as those whose parents did not use the baby vernacular as frequently." (Boggs, 2017)

The shorter version: speaking to babies in their language helps them learn adult language faster. Pretty amazing! So keep up those lunchtime conversations - they're good for the baby's brain *and* for bonding!

Learning

When my oldest was about seven months old, I knew it was time. I ceremoniously sat her down on my lap, grabbed my delicate childhood copy of Maurice Sendak's *Where the Wild Things Are,* and began to read. I was so excited to finally share my favorite childhood story with her. After all, she was old enough to eat real food, so surely she could sit through a very short book.

By page three, I surrendered. She was trying to tear the pages and throwing a fit because I wouldn't let her.

Don't make the same mistake I did, but don't lose hope, either! While reading full-length children's books is a no-go at this age, board books are perfect for the six-month crowd. Select books that have high-quality, colorful images and not a lot of text. Remember: the goal is *not* to read your baby a story. The goal is to show her images of real-life objects she can learn to relate to. Now is not the time for Dr. Seuss, fairy tales, or, heaven forbid, Leo Tolstoy.

Here are some qualities to look for in board books at this stage:

- Simple, bright photos
- Good color contrast
- Not a lot of words

As you can see, it's best to keep it simple. And remember, your baby is not interested in a long-winded story. He'll be much more interested in grabbing, biting, and throwing the board books. That's why they're made of relatively indestructible cardboard, so it's best to just accept this reality and move on.

・ ・ ・

Keeping Baby Safe

My partner and I were getting a little frustrated. We were first-time parents living in a small apartment, and our daughter was into everything. She even started to throw massive fits when she couldn't open the drawers at her level. We couldn't even watch a 45-minute TV show or work on the computer in silence while she was awake. She was unstoppable and relentless.

In a stroke of genius, we figured out a new solution: instead of keeping our daughter out of all these spaces she wanted to explore, why not make them accessible and safe?

Your baby will be more and more mobile in the coming months - and her curiosity will also increase. Take a walk around the house and see if there are any spaces at her level that you could allow her to explore. For example, we moved all our lightweight, plastic dishes into a lower cabinet and put the kitchen appliances up high, then removed the child locks. Instead of having a screaming fit when she couldn't open the door, our daughter would entertain herself safely and learn all about Tupperware in the meantime. And my partner and I could eat dinner in peace. Win-win!

Of course, there are limits to this method, and it might result in more dishes, but if the baby's happy, everyone's happy!

How is Mom?

As your baby's feeding needs change and you introduce more solid foods, your partner might experience pain while breastfeeding. This might be alarming, especially if nursing has been smooth sailing up to this point.

There are a couple of common culprits when it comes to breastfeeding difficulties, but these are the big three:

- Clogged ducts
- Thrush

- Mastitis

Here's a bit of info about each of these problems, as well as some simple ways to alleviate the pain.

Clogged Ducts: This is basically a blockage that can occur when your partner stops nursing as frequently or is stressed or fatigued. It's common to get clogged ducts right around the return to the workplace, which may have happened recently for your partner. Clogged ducts are also common when the baby stops nursing as much as at night. Tight clothing and underwire bras can also contribute.

Clogged ducts are painful, but with sleep, hydration, and regular emptying of the breast, they usually resolve on their own. Encourage your partner to nurse as much as possible and take some time to rest. She can also massage her breast toward the nipple as she is nursing or pumping to encourage milk flow.

Mastitis: Mastitis is more commonly known as a breast infection. It's basically clogged ducts on steroids. In addition to the clogged duct symptoms, your partner will develop flu-like symptoms and generally feel horrible.

My partner has struggled with mastitis a lot in the past, so I feel like I have a good handle on it. Here are my top three tips for dealing with mastitis:

1. Don't Wait. If your partner has the symptoms of clogged ducts and also spikes a fever, she should go in right away so she can get on antibiotics promptly. If she waits too long, the infection could turn into an abscess.
2. Sleep and Hydrate. Encourage your partner to rest for a full day (at least!) and hydrate throughout the day.
3. Nurse as Much as Possible. The more she keeps the milk flowing, the less likely she is to develop a severe infection.

Thrush: Have you heard of yeast infections? The same fungus that is responsible for those nasty infections can cause another condition known as thrush. The name sounds scary, and I'll be frank: if you don't catch it early, it can be a little nightmarish.

The reason thrush is such a pain is that it often infects both the mom *and* the baby. It's also extremely contagious, so watch out for yourself.

The symptoms of thrush include nipple pain, red or peeling nipples, cracked or sore nipples, and a burning feeling while breastfeeding (or in general). Your baby might be unusually fussy, or he could have white patches in his mouth. Your partner might also have a vaginal yeast infection. As I said, it's not very pleasant!

If your partner or baby has recently been on antibiotics, thrush might be even more likely. You're also at higher risk if you have diabetes.

The good news is thrush can be treated with anti fungal medications. If your partner's symptoms last more than a week, she should consult with her physician.

One big tip for preventing all these conditions: practice self-care and try not to stress. More on that next.

How is Dad?

Just like your partner, stress relief is crucial for happy parenting. At this point, the science is undeniable: stress causes sickness, decreased performance at work, and increased rates of depression and anxiety.

Of course, it's impossible to eliminate all stressors from our lives. What you can control is how you respond to stress and how you take care of yourself. In the busyness of being a new dad, don't forget to manage your stress. How can you do that successfully? Here are a few ideas:

- Reach out to friends and family and get together. You don't have to stop socializing now that you're a dad - in fact, now it's more important than ever.
- Get out of the house. Go for a walk in nature, to a sports game, or just sit outside. Studies show that sunlight and a change in scenery go a long way in preventing depression and coping with stress.
- Seek counseling or professional help if you can't shake the stressed feeling. There's a fine line between stress and depression, and if you're experiencing the latter, it's important to get help.
- Be active. Physical activity is another great way to channel stress. If there was a type of exercise or sport you enjoyed before your baby was born and things got hectic, get back into it!

Most importantly, communicate with your partner. If you feel overwhelmed by stress, don't keep it to yourself. Not only is it bad for you, but your partner will probably notice you're not being open - with causes even more stress!

Despite the fun moments and baby laughs, months 6 and 7 can be a little challenging when you throw teething and growth spurts in the mix. Congratulations on making it through!

CHAPTER 8
READY, SET, GO!

 "Having kids is like living in a frat house -- nobody sleeps, everything's broken, and there's a lot of throwing up." -- Ray Romano

Your Baby's Milestones: Months 8 and 9			
Eating	**Sleeping**	**Motor Skills**	**Language**
Good time to introduce sippy cup Drink about 24 ounces per day	Sleeps an average of 12-15 hours per day Decreases to 2 naps per day instead of 3	Throws things for fun Might start to pull up on furniture	Babbles Points to objects Might be able to learn basic baby sign

MONTH 8

YOU'VE LEARNED a lot about your baby over the last two months, and you've probably also persevered through some challenging moments. Now it's time to get ready for crawling, pulling up on furniture, and playtime.

Feeding

Your baby will become increasingly independent at mealtime over the next few months, but make sure you're still there to supervise. In addition to the foods I've already discussed, here are a few items to add to the baby's menu this month:

- Yogurt (plain, made with whole milk)
- Dry cereal designed for babies
- Small pieces of tofu

This is also a great month to introduce the sippy cup. If your baby is already taking a bottle regularly, this should be a pretty smooth transition. If your partner is exclusively breastfeeding and the baby hasn't taken a bottle, it might require a bit of practice.

Here are some qualities to look for in a starter sippy cup:

- Easy for baby to hold
- Soft mouthpiece
- Spout that resembles a nipple for exclusively breastfeeding babies
- Spill-proof!

Breastmilk and formula should still make up the majority of your baby's calories at this age, but feel free to let your baby have water in the sippy cup. Hold off on cow's milk and juice for now. (If you're wondering, babies this age can have yogurt even though it is made from cow's milk because it is cultured, making it easier to digest.)

Finally, remember that if your baby doesn't take to the sippy cup right away, it's not a big deal. Most doctors don't recommend phasing out bottles completely until babies are twelve months old, so you still have time!

Sleeping

Once again, your baby might go through a sleep regression this month or next. As her body adjusts to eating solids, cutting teeth, and being more active - not to mention all the huge mental jumps her brain is going through - it's understandable that sleep patterns might become unpredictable.

For example, if your baby has been taking three naps up to this point, expect that to decrease to two at some point soon. As far as nighttime is concerned, don't be alarmed if your baby wakes much more frequently this month. In fact, it might be best to just get a head start and plan a night-time feeding/comforting strategy with your partner before the sleeping difficulties hit.

And of course, keep in mind it's okay for the baby to cry at night. But if you feel inclined to comfort him, that's okay, too. Giving the baby a sippy cup with some water to keep in the crib might help him self-soothe. Just avoid giving him juice or breastmilk, which can cause tooth decay.

Bonding With Baby

As I've mentioned before, communicating with your baby is one of the best bonding activities you can do at this stage of development - and for your child's whole life. Open communication builds trust between kids and parents, and it really does start from the beginning.

One way to communicate more easily with your baby is to learn some simple baby signs. Baby sign language certainly isn't necessary for your baby to learn, but in my experience, it can make things much simpler, especially at feeding time. My partner and I haven't used baby sign language extensively, but we do teach our babies the following five signs around this age:

1. "Drink": Make a cup with your hand and pretend to be drinking it
2. "Water": Tuck your thumb and pinkie in like you're making the number "3," then tap your chin with your index finger
3. "More": Babies are always quick to pick up on this one! Pinch your fingers against your thumb on both hands. With the fingers facing each other, tap both hands together repeatedly.
4. "Milk": Pump both hands like you're milking a cow. Yep, it's that simple.
5. "All done": Put your hands in front of you with the palms forward, the switch to palms facing you, and repeat.

And of course, this is a great age to start with the classic signs we all know, like "bye-bye" and "blow a kiss"!

EAT   DRINK   MORE

Learning

There's a special moment that happens at this age, and it is really remarkable. Picture this: you're holding your baby, and she drops her toy on the ground. Not too exciting up to this point, right? You just pick it up and give it back to her and move on.

Not anymore. Now, if you pick it up and give it back to her, she'll probably throw it right back on the floor and squeal with delight. Your little girl has learned an entertaining activity: dropping things!

Once the charm has worn off, you might think your little one is dropping things just to drive you insane, but her motives aren't that sinister. She's really just honing a new skill, the same way she has been practicing pinching objects, picking things up, rolling, and babbling. Humans learn through repetition, and this month she's getting a great lesson in object permanence.

Keeping Baby Safe

If you've kept up with the childproofing tips so far, you should be pretty set this month. But if your baby is slithering, crawling, or doing whatever variation he likes best, you've probably noticed he's a lot dirtier than he was in his squeaky-clean newborn days! That's because he's spending a lot more time on the floor.

Here are some tips for keeping the floor safe and clean now that your baby is exploring every nook and cranny:

- Buy a robot vacuum - or put it on your wish list if you have family members who want to buy you a great, practical Christmas present.
- Lie a clean sheet down on the floor in the room where your baby is crawling or scooting around. Put the corners of the sheet under coffee tables or other heavy furniture to secure them in place.

- Dress your baby in pants or leg warmers to protect his knees and keep him cleaner.

You might worry that the floor is unsafe or too dirty for your baby. Rest assured, some research shows these initial floor-dwelling months are good for your baby's immune system and could even prevent asthma later in life.

How is Mom?

There's a lot of talk out there about babies who have separation anxiety, but not as many people realize that it can also happen to moms. One study by the Society for Research in Child Development found that maternal separation often peaks when babies are around this age.

Maternal separation anxiety is exactly what it sounds like: an intense feeling of worry, fear, or guilt when mom is separated from the baby. Your partner might also experience irritability, fatigue, and even physical symptoms like nausea, headaches, and panic attacks. It can be debilitating in severe cases, so it's important that your partner gets help if she has symptoms.

If your partner shows symptoms of maternal separation anxiety, communicate with her openly and non-judgmentally. Reassure her that it's normal to feel stressed and worried about the baby, but also suggest that she discuss her symptoms with her care provider. Counseling and medical interventions can make an amazing difference.

How is Dad?

If you haven't gone out on a date since your baby was born, now is the time. Your baby can probably take a bottle at this point, and might even be eating solid food. But even if that's not the case, breastfeeding frequency should have spaced out enough to go out for dinner with your partner.

That's all well and good, but there's probably a big question on your mind: who's going to watch the baby? If you don't have family or friends who could do it, ask around about trusted babysitters. Make sure you get a chance to meet the sitter beforehand since this will allow you and your partner to be more at ease.

When date night comes around, have the sitter come about 15 minutes before you want to leave so you can show her around the house, explain any feeding needs, and show her exactly how you put the baby down. The trick with babysitters is to keep things as normal as possible, so give the sitter a full debrief of all your routines.

That's a wrap on month eight. Hopefully, you've enjoyed a date night with your partner and maybe even learned some baby sign language with your little one. On to the last three months of year one!

MONTH 9

Your baby has officially been outside the womb as long as he or she was inside it. A lot can happen in just nine months! Nine months might actually be my favorite baby stage - and not just because nine is my favorite number. Your baby is really blossoming, and now that you've gotten through some of the growth spurts, teething struggles, and general insecurity of new parenthood, you'll love watching the changes take place.

Feeding

This month is a great time to start putting utensils on the baby's tray. Your baby is probably already showing interest in using the same dishes, spoons, and forks as mom and dad, anyway. I remember our fourth child refused to eat unless his highchair tray was set in the exact same configuration as mine and his mom's!

Before I go on, here is a disclaimer: just because you give your baby a spoon and fork does not mean he or she will be able to use them. In fact, it will probably be quite some time before the baby is eating with utensils in a civilized way. So don't put away the bibs and spill mats just yet!

That said, allowing the baby to practice - or really, play - with utensils during meal times is a great way to encourage fine motor skill development. Here are some tips for getting started:

- Buy utensils that are designed for young babies. The best materials are silicone or BPA-free plastic (metal is a bit heavier and best for when the baby is older). The utensils should be light enough for the baby to easily hold, and they should be much smaller than normal utensils.
- Serve foods that won't be too frustrating for the baby. The best foods are ones with a thicker texture that doesn't slide off the spoon, like mashed chickpeas or mashed sweet potatoes.
- Prepare for messiness. Lots of messiness. Once your baby figures out how to get the food on the spoon or fork, don't be surprised if he would rather draw on his tray than actually eat. Expect most of the food *not* to make it into his mouth.
- Keep the servings small. (See previous note - the less food you serve, the less mess!)

As for plates, personally, I prefer to skip them. There's a much higher chance the baby will actually throw the food *out* of the highchair zone if you serve it on a plate. Just put a tablespoon or two directly on the highchair tray, hand the baby his utensils, and let him have some fun.

Looking for new foods to add to your baby's repertoire? We usually introduce meat around the nine-month mark, and it always goes over well. Shredded chicken and ground beef are some great options. Just make sure the meat is well-cooked and then allowed to cool enough for your baby to handle.

. . .

Sleeping

My one important note this month: check in with your baby's crib mattress. If your baby is starting to pull up on furniture (more on that below), it's probably time to lower your baby's mattress. Once your baby can pull up on furniture that is about eye level, it makes sense that the guardrail should be higher than that.

Another note: if you've been co-sleeping with your baby until this point, this is a good time to introduce a separate sleeping space. Try a co-sleeper that fits up next to your bed, or put a crib next to you.

Finally, my last word of advice is to trust your parental instincts. Different parents feel different ways about sleeping arrangements at this point, and for good reason: we all have different situations regarding work, sleep, and emotional status. Take all these factors into account as you choose the best solution for your family.

Bonding With Baby

To this day, one of my favorite ways to bond with my oldest child - now age fourteen - is by playing games. We love to go to a nearby board game cafe and check out a few board games to play. There's something about games that provides the perfect bonding opportunity: problem-solving, laughter, and friendly competition.

Of course, at this age, competition isn't really a factor, but playing games with your baby is one of the best ways to bond. It's surprising how much a nine-month-old baby can actually participate in play. Here are some fun games to try with your little guy or gal:

- **Peek-a-boo:** The classic, and for good reason - babies love it!
- **How big is baby:** Say, "How big is [insert name here]?" And then reply, "Soooo big!" while waving your hands in the air.
- **Chase the baby:** Pretend to be a bear and chase your baby around the room while pretending to eat her toes.

- **Hide the toy:** Same object permanence concept as peek-a-boo, but with a toy.
- **Dance party:** Turn on music and dance around the room.

The interactive aspect of play makes it a great bonding activity, but as a bonus, it's also amazing for your baby's brain development. As usual, the things that help your baby bond with you also help with physical and neurological development. It's a win-win for both of you!

Learning

This month, it's time for your baby's 9-month checkup. In addition to measurements (no vaccines at this appointment if you've kept up so far), your pediatrician might ask about the following developmental milestones:

- Can your baby sit without support?
- Does your baby grasp objects and get mad if an object is taken away?
- Does your baby crawl or stand while holding onto a stable object/person?
- Does your baby mimic you?
- Does your baby point to indicate what she wants?
- Does your baby babble? (Make consonant sounds like "mama," "baba," and "dada"?)

Keeping Baby Safe

In addition to all the physical and neurological changes your baby is going through this month, you might also notice a big step: cruising. This basically means your baby will start pulling up on furniture (she may be doing this already), then walking from side to side, using the furniture as support.

This might seem like a small thing, but it's a huge step! Walking could be just around the corner, or it could still be quite a way off. Either way, it's important to encourage this important stage of development and also keep your baby safe. Here are some tips:

- Get ready for some spills. Now that baby is upright, it's inevitable that he or she will have some falls. Don't beat yourself up if and when it happens!
- Make sure all your furniture is secured to the wall. Babies will pull up on anything within reach, and it's easier than you might think for furniture to tip!
- Get on baby's level - literally. The best way to find safety hazards is to crawl around the house and inspect everything at the baby's eye level. Remove any dangerous objects as you come across them, and secure any furniture that might be hazardous.
- Follow your baby. When in doubt, just put your baby down on the ground and observe what she does for about thirty minutes. This will give you a good idea of what you might need to babyproof.

Your baby's increased mobility is exciting, but it can also be a little nerve-wracking. Remember, when your baby is in sight, you're doing all right. But for the moments you or your partner can't be present, it's reassuring to know your home is safe for exploration.

A final note: if your baby isn't cruising yet, don't worry. As I've said before - every baby is different! In the meantime, it doesn't hurt to get a head start on babyproofing since it could happen at any time.

How is Mom?

The 9-month mark seems like it would bring freedom from the effects of pregnancy and childbirth, but that's not always the case. If your partner feels discouraged that she isn't "back to normal" at this point, you can both rest assured that this is totally normal.

Whatever you do, don't trust the Internet, which will tell your partner she should "bounce back" between 6 and 12 weeks (that was like, 6 months ago, right?) While she's probably not dealing with any of the more acute postpartum symptoms - the ones everyone talks about, like bleeding, engorgement, pelvic floor soreness, or post-cesarean abdominal scar healing - there are likely to be other lingering effects of what her body has gone through over the last eighteen months. Some of these include:

- Difficulty losing weight
- Fatigue
- Stretch marks
- Saggy skin on her belly
- Leaking urine during high-impact activity
- Discomfort during intercourse

While these symptoms are normal, they can still be disheartening. Encourage your partner to discuss any concerns with her care provider, and give her lots of affirmation if she is struggling. Nine months might seem like a long time, but childbirth is a demanding process that requires more healing time than what the common opinion dictates.

How is Dad?

Around this month, I start establishing a routine with my kids. If there are periods of time when I'm the sole source of entertainment (and, of course, food), I try to get the baby excited to spend time with me. I know that sounds kind of sad, but if Mom needs to leave the house, it can be hard to convince the baby to be happy!

Now that your baby is more interactive, I have a word of advice: start to build your "dad bag." This is a bag (or actually, I use a plastic bin) of toys, random objects, and snacks that only come out when it's my turn to babysit. When your partner has to work on weekends, and you're home with the baby, you can bring out the dad bag, and rest assured your baby will be quickly distracted from mom's absence.

Some ideas for things to put in the dad bag at this age:

- Finger foods the baby doesn't usually get (for example, I have a few containers of puffed cereal and some applesauce pouches)
- Electronic toys that the baby doesn't play with often (my partner can't stand electronic toys - her loss!)
- Sensory blocks
- Some dad-time board books that we always read together

This is a trick that will work throughout most of your baby's early childhood. Our "baby" is now 18 months old, and I still have a dad bag for days when my partner has to work, and we don't have childcare. Give it a try!

Nine months postpartum is hopefully less difficult than nine months pregnant - but no matter what, you're making it through this first year and getting to know your baby (and your partner) as you go. Not to mention, you've probably learned a few new things about yourself.

CHAPTER 9
BYE BYE BABY

 "Until you have a son of your own, you will never know the joy, the love beyond feeling that resonates in the heart of a father as he looks upon his son." – Kent Nerburn

Your Baby's Milestones: Months 10 and 11			
Eating	Sleeping	Motor Skills	Language
Eats about 16-24 ounces per day Eats most simple baby foods Might start to wean off bottle	Might cut back to one long nap per day Sleeps about 14 hours per day	Starts to cruise Sees an object across the room and goes to it	Can say "mama" or "dada" Points to objects when you name them

MONTH 10

ONCE OUR KIDS have hit the ten-month mark, I feel like they have a very limited amount of time left as a baby. Toddlerhood is just around the corner, and the last three months of the first year are a time of remarkable changes. Here's what to expect from your little one this month.

Feeding

At this point, your baby can eat pretty much anything, but you should still hold off on the following foods:

- Cow's milk
- Honey
- Dried fruit and nuts
- Raw vegetables and fruits that pose a choking hazard
- Highly processed foods that are high in sodium and sugar

Just like most things in your baby's life, creating a meal schedule for your baby will help establish consistent, healthy habits. It also makes it easier for you if you need to leave your baby with a caregiver. Here's a sample menu for a 10-month-old, along with some health benefits for each food.

Breakfast:

- Scrambled egg: An amazing source of protein, healthy fats, and nutrients
- Banana: Great source of potassium and healthy carbohydrates

Lunch:

- Cubed, cooked sweet potato: Lots of fiber and vitamins
- Soft cheese: Cottage cheese is a healthy option that is rich in calcium

Snack:

- Yogurt (plain, made with whole milk): Full of probiotics for gut health

Dinner:

- Diced chicken: Good protein source
- White rice: Simple carbs that are easy to digest
- Applesauce: A healthy dessert!

As you can see, your baby eats most of the same foods you do at this point. You can keep things really simple by just feeding your baby the same meals you and your partner eat, if possible. Just make sure to dice any foods that might be a choking hazard and allow hot foods to cool completely before serving them to your baby.

Sleeping

Sleep habits tend to become a little more reliable from here on out - which is great news! Your baby might cut back from two naps to one long nap this month. Generally speaking, if your baby still naps two times per day, you can expect him to take the first nap after about four hours of being awake, then the second nap about three hours after the first. Bedtime should be about four or five hours after the baby wakes up from a second nap.

Your baby will probably nap for about two or three hours per day, with eleven or twelve hours of sleep at night.

Here's an example of what your baby's sleep might look like this month:

- 7:00: Wake
- 10:30 - 12:00: First nap
- 2:30 - 3:30: Second nap

- 6:30: Start bedtime routine (bath, read a book, change diaper, pajamas)
- 7:00: Bedtime

But remember, nothing is set in stone at this age and sleep patterns are variable, so try to be flexible and expect the unexpected!

Bonding With Baby

Now that your baby is becoming more and more independent, you might think you don't need to hold her as much. But physical contact and affection remain important ways to strengthen your bond. If your baby seems fussy, restless, or just plain grouchy, and you've tried food, sleep, diaper changes, and teething remedies, it might be that she simply wants to cuddle. Don't underestimate the power of snuggling!

Baby wearing can also come in handy here. My babies really enjoyed it when I wore them on my back at this age. This allows the baby to look out and see the world while he's awake and energetic and then rest his head on your back when he gets worn out.

Learning

Ten-month-old babies are extremely curious and usually pretty fearless too, which can keep mom and dad on their toes! Learning at this age happens primarily by engagement with all five senses, whether that be through play, eating, or just exploring. Here are some ways to engage each of your baby's five senses this month and help with his or her cognitive development:

Sight: It's hard to believe that just ten months ago, your baby could only see a few feet in front of her and was unable to track movement. Her vision has improved drastically since then, and now she can spot her favorite sippy cup from across the room and rapidly move to go grab it.

Engage baby's sense of sight by continuing to read board books with clear pictures (photographs are great at this age) and lots of color contrast.

Sound: You might have noticed your baby responding to the sound of music, or swaying to a good beat. Babies love music, and it's amazing for their brain development. A 2016 study showed that listening to music helps the baby's speech development. Pretty amazing!

You don't have to subject yourself to Baby Mozart, either. Our children have loved a variety of music at this age, from classical, to bluegrass, to reggae. Anything with a strong beat is sure to get baby dancing!

Smell/Taste: It's easy to take the sense of smell for granted, but it might be our strongest sense at birth. Newborn babies are able to recognize their caregiver's scent and recognize them, which compensates for the lack of vision in those early days.

The best way to develop a baby's sense of smell and taste is to expose him to a wide variety of healthy foods. Encourage him to smell his food before he tastes it. I've done this with all our kids, and it's amazing to see how much it helps them be comfortable trying new foods. When you're cooking, keep baby close by and give her different ingredients to smell, like garlic, onions, and herbs. You'll probably get some funny reactions!

Touch: The sense of touch is the very first sense to develop in the womb. At age ten months, your baby's sense of touch helps her learn about dimension and space. You might notice your baby touches your face if you sit face-to-face with her at a close distance. This is her way of getting to know you better, and it applies to the whole world (hence the need to babyproof everything!).

This month, encourage your baby to learn through her sense of touch by providing objects with different textures. Babies also love putting things in containers at this age and stacking blocks. It doesn't have to be fancy to be developmentally beneficial!

Keeping Baby Safe

Childproofing is important and good, but the best way to keep your child safe in the world is to teach them how not to get hurt. Up to this point, that's been pretty hard to do, but with your baby's new speech development, you can begin to teach him how to stay safe.

Babies of this age form strong associations between sounds and situations. Use this to your advantage when teaching your baby about safety. For example, when you're in the kitchen, point to the stove and say "Ouch" or "Hot" while making a serious (not mad or angry!) face. Or if your baby starts to crawl close to the stairs, don't just run over and pick him up. Instead, calmly pick him up and say "Ouch" in a stern voice, then explain why he shouldn't play by the stairs. These simple communications will instruct your baby about what is and isn't safe.

But of course, he is still a baby - so don't stop with the babyproofing just yet!

How is Mom?

I'll never forget something that happened after our first baby was born. She was around this age, and my partner was just recovering from a horrible bout of mastitis. She had been nursing literally around the clock and was totally exhausted. At one point, she seemed really down, so I asked if there was anything I could do for her. She thought about it for a minute and then said, "I think I just need to go on a walk outside for like, five minutes..by myself."

I thought she was joking at first, but then I realized that between taking care of the baby, resting, and working, she hadn't really had any time to just *be*. She was so caught up in all the items on the to-do list that she had literally forgotten about herself. I realized I needed to give her more space to do things she enjoyed, like being outdoors, reading, running, and gardening. I needed to make sure she prioritized her own needs.

Now that your baby is more independent encourage your partner to take some time for herself once a week. This could be going out with a friend, doing a hobby she enjoys, playing a sport, or any other enjoyable activity. The first year of motherhood can be hard for some women, as their sense of identity becomes more and more bound up with the baby. Taking time for herself will help her recharge and regain her sense of self.

How is Dad?

There's a lot of talk about when moms should start exercising after childbirth, but what about the dads? Like so many dads out there, you might have been so caught up in your new baby, work, and your relationship with your partner that you've let yourself go a little bit. Ever heard of "dad bod"? Yeah, it happens. But that's okay. It's never too late to get back to it!

If you're like me, you might find yourself interested in exercise for the first time in your life now that your baby is here. I wasn't into sports growing up, but after my daughter was born, something clicked. Suddenly I got into soccer, running, and weightlifting. This had a huge effect not only on my relationship with my baby and my partner but on my life. I was more confident and energetic and felt more in control of my health and well-being.

This month, why not try out a gym membership? Most gyms offer a free trial period that allows you to scope out the place and try any classes you might be interested in. Just like your partner, you have to make sure to carve out time for yourself, and a trip to the gym might be just the ticket.

Parenthood isn't just about the baby: it's about you, your partner, the baby, and your relationship. This month, try to slow down and enjoy these people you call family. Cancel some plans you've been dreading anyways, and stay home for a movie night with your people. No one's going to complain about that!

MONTH 11

Next month, your baby turns one! If you're planning a birthday party, this is the month to get a head start on preparations. Take some time to sit down with your partner early in the month and nail down the following details:

1. Party date, time, and location
2. Guest list
3. Food or drink you will serve
4. Presents!
5. Invitations

It's best to send out invitations about two weeks in advance to give people plenty of time to plan, or three weeks if you are sending physical invitations. Even though the party isn't until next month, the more work you do this month, the more you'll be able to sit back and enjoy the day.

Feeding

It might seem like your independent guy or gal doesn't need breastmilk or formula anymore, but you should still be feeding 16 to 24 ounces per day. Aside from that, real food is increasingly the name of the game. However, some pediatricians do recommend parents start weaning the baby off the bottle at this age. That might seem like an impossible task, but with planning and consistency, you can do it.

Here are a few steps to weaning your baby from the bottle this month:

1. Offer the sippy cup for the baby's first feeding. If you catch him when he's hungry, he's more likely to take to the sippy cup.
2. Once you've successfully replaced the bottle for the first feeding, add in one sippy cup feeding per day. I like to switch off and on - so first feeding with the sippy, second feeding with the bottle, third sippy, etc.
3. Continue this pattern until your baby is completely weaned from the bottle.

Consistency is the key here. Your baby might not like it for a few days, but just like with sleep training, a consistent routine will produce good results. Make sure that you offer the sippy cup at the same time every day. And remember, this does not apply to nursing from the breast, which should continue for at least one year. We'll discuss this more below!

Sleeping

There's so much pressure in the parenting world for your baby to sleep all night, which can make parents feel like they're doing something wrong if their baby still wakes at night. Instead of obsessing over that long night-time stretch of sleep (as nice as it is when it happens!), try to get in touch with your baby's sleep habits. One of the best ways to do this is by keeping a baby sleep journal.

A baby sleep journal is exactly what it sounds like: a written record of when your baby sleeps and wakes. My partner and I have kept sleep journals at various points in our kids' lives - usually when we're having struggles. But even at non-challenging times, it's a great way to get a better sense of your baby's habits.

Keeping a sleep journal allows you to pay close attention to when your baby's waking hours are, and how long the stretches usually last. This can be a game-changer when it comes to baby sleep. For example, if your baby is fighting nap time (as babies often do at this age), try taking notes every day for a week about how long your baby tends to stay awake between sleep times. This will allow you to see if you might need to extend the waking window or not. If you discover you have been trying to put your baby down for a nap after a two-hour waking window, try waiting 2.5 or 3 hours and see if that makes it more peaceful. Sometimes, making these minor adjustments can make sleep much less of a struggle.

By age 11 months, your baby might not be sleeping through the night, but hopefully, you have at least gotten a better sense of a sleep pattern. If you still feel completely frustrated and confused by your baby's sleep habits, a sleep journal should get you on the track to feeling more in control.

Bonding With Baby

Continuing the trend from previous months, this month offers a lot of opportunities for the #1 bonding activity: communication. You'll notice your baby is gesturing a lot more to communicate his needs. For example, he might point and grunt at his bottle from across the room or toddle over to you and stretch out his arms to ask to be picked up. Whether you can fulfill his request or not, make sure you give him a response. This will teach him that he can trust you to listen to him and respond to his needs. It will also teach him *to* communicate in the first place!

Here are some other communication skills your baby might develop (with your help!) this month:

- Babbling in "conversation"
- Grunting in response to a question or to indicate a desire
- Pointing at objects
- Following simple directions
- Saying "mama," "dada," "baba" and other simple words

And there's another means of communication your baby might develop this month: the art of the temper tantrum. Don't be alarmed! I find the best way to calm a tantrum at this age is just to hold the baby and provide comfort while the baby calms down. It can be difficult to figure out the causes of tantrums at this age, so usually, removing the baby from the environment and providing some TLC will de-escalate the situation.

Learning

Develop your baby's language skills this month by naming objects and describing processes. She might not be able to say many words, but you've probably noticed that she understands a lot!

One of my favorite learning activities to do with my kids at this age was to take them on walks. Leave your phone at home and step outside for some fresh air and a little language exercise. Some of the simplest words to teach your baby - "sky," "tree," "bird," "airplane," "car" - are right outside your door. And of course, your baby will love the walking practice! If you can't get outside, you can also do this activity at the window. If your window faces a street, your baby will love watching the cars go by.

And of course, keep up the reading! At this age, your baby might even start to pick board books up and "read" them by herself. Again, even though she can't vocalize the words yet, her brain is absorbing so much, just with the visual stimulation.

Finally, encourage learning by posing a lot of questions. At mealtime, ask your baby if she would like one food or another. For example, "Do you want yogurt or cereal?" She might not be able to provide an answer yet, but she's on the way! This month she might even nod "yes" or shake her head "no" in response to questions. This is an exciting parenting moment - you can finally communicate a little bit more!

. . .

Keeping Baby Safe

Now that the baby is probably on his feet a lot more, make sure you always check the surfaces he is walking on. I remember one time I took my daughter to the playground and wondered why she wouldn't walk on the pavement. Then I realized it was super hot, and she was only wearing socks!

You might also consider getting some lightweight shoes for your baby to wear to protect his feet. Baby moccasins are a great choice because they stay on better than a lot of other options. At this age, your baby doesn't need tennis shoes with thick soles - in fact, the more flexible the sole, the better.

How is Mom?

If most of your partner's friends don't have kids yet, this can be a lonely time - especially if she is staying home with the baby full-time. Encourage her to look for local groups of parents that she can connect with. Not only will this provide your baby with a great opportunity for play dates, but perhaps more importantly, it will allow your partner to get some much-needed social time with other moms who understand the challenges and joys of raising babies.

If your partner has struggled with postpartum depression, this is all the more important. Research has shown that women are much more likely to experience postpartum depression when they don't have social support. There are many support groups that are designed specifically for moms who are working through postpartum depression, so encourage your partner to ask your local hospital or medical health professional for resources to get the support she needs.

How is Dad?

Low social support is also a risk factor for paternal postpartum depression, so my advice this month for you is the same as it was for your partner - find your people! Get together with a dad friend, or look for social support groups in your area if you feel the need to socialize. There are also many couple support groups that offer opportunities for friendship and support as you adjust to your life as new parents.

Even if you're not struggling with depression or other mental health symptoms, getting together with a friend can be a real fresh of breath air when you've been talking baby talk all day. So set aside some time this month for socialization!

Now that your baby is entering the early stages of toddlerhood, parenting becomes both easier and more difficult. On the one hand, your baby is more independent and not as reliant on you and your partner. On the other hand, there are a lot more decisions to be made! What parenting style is the best fit for you? What do you envision for your baby's education or activities in the future?

Of course, you have plenty of time to think about all this, but it's pretty exciting to see your little one's increasing personality and to imagine what he or she will be like at this time next year - not to mention five years from now.

CHAPTER 10
FIRST BIRTHDAY

 "Nothing ever fits the palm so perfectly, or feels so right, or inspires so much protective instinct as the hand of a child." – Gregory David Roberts

Your Baby's Milestones: Month 12			
Eating	**Sleeping**	**Motor Skills**	**Language**
Eats about 16-24 ounces per day Can start to drink cow's milk	Sleeps an average of 13-14 hours per day Takes at least one nap per day	Might start walking independently	Says "no" Says at least one word that designates a specific object

FEEDING

At this age, one of the best ways to calm a restless baby is to put him in his high chair with his favorite finger foods. Then again, your baby might also start to show some signs of pickiness at this age. Just when you thought you had the least picky baby on the block, he'll start throwing what you thought was his favorite food yesterday on the floor today. Don't fret - it's classic! Just continue to offer a variety of nutritious, healthy foods about 3-5 times per day.

This month, your baby can finally try out cow's milk. Don't get too excited, though - a lot of babies can't stand it at first. Start with a very small amount - a tablespoon added to formula or breastmilk or formula is fine at first. Make sure your baby tolerates the milk well before you increase the amount. Here are some signs that he's not quite ready for cow's milk:

- Swollen lips, face, or eyes
- Itchy rash
- Digestive issues like vomiting, diarrhea, or cramping
- Runny nose
- Eczema
- Diaper rash

If your baby starts displaying these symptoms shortly after cow's milk is introduced, that might be a clue that it is related to the milk. Talk to your pediatrician about these symptoms before you continue to give your baby cow's milk.

Sleeping

Your baby seems like she's all grown up these days, but she still needs 13-14 hours of sleep every day. That usually looks like 2-3 hours of napping during the day and 10-11 hours of nighttime sleep.

Make sure you don't skip the bedtime routine at this age. Your little one has gotten used to the rhythm of each day, and even though she might fight bedtime more than she did last month, she really needs the ritual of a bedtime routine.

If you haven't sleep-trained your baby yet, you might wonder if it's too late. The answer is, of course not! Just keep in mind that many babies go through a growth spurt around this age, so it's normal for sleep patterns to be a bit off. This also might make it more difficult to sleep-train your baby, but with consistency, you will see results.

Bonding With Baby

Your baby might have learned a very important and fun word by now: "no." You might wonder how you're going to deal when she's saying no on a regular basis! A lot of parents start wondering about discipline at this age, and it's no wonder! Toddlers can be pretty stubborn and headstrong.

So why am I discussing discipline in the bonding section? Because discipline without bonding is a dead end. Forming a strong bond of trust with your baby is the first step in establishing effective discipline. This foundation of trust continues to be important through toddlerhood, elementary school, and even in the teenage years. It all starts now!

Here are some tips for successful discipline and trust establishment at this age:

1. Breathe before you react. Stop and take three deep breaths before you take action. This gives you some time to clear your head and respond in a gentle, loving way.
2. Establish boundaries. All that babyproofing you've done plays an important part in discipline from a young age since it establishes areas that are off-limits.
3. Be consistent. This is the hardest and most critical step, but experts agree consistency is key to discipline at any age.

Keep in mind that disciplining your child is an act of love. For me, it helps to think of discipline as instruction and teaching instead of simply bossing your child around.

Learning

Your baby will have her one-year checkup this month. In addition to the usual physical checkup items like vaccinations, height and weight check, and head measurements, your doctor will also ask you about the following learning milestones:

- Is your child saying any words?
- Does your child respond to simple instructions and the word "No"?
- Is your child pulling up on furniture and cruising?
- Has your child started walking yet?
- Does your child play simple games like peek-a-boo?

Generally at this age, your answer to most of these questions will probably be yes. Talk to your pediatrician at the appointment if you have any concerns about learning milestones or language development. Early intervention is key, so an open discussion will allow your care provider to address any problems early on.

Keeping Baby Safe

Now that your baby is bigger and more mobile, you might wonder if it's safe to move his car seat to a forward-facing position. Although the recommendation used to be one year, the American Academy of Pediatrics now recommends that toddlers stay rear-facing until they are at least two years of age.

To make your baby more comfortable, consider switching to a convertible car seat if you haven't already. Convertible car seats have a bit more space, making them more comfortable - especially for long car rides. Generally, it is recommended to switch to a convertible car seat when the top of your child's head is less than an inch from the top of his infant car seat or when she is 30 inches tall or 30 pounds. For most toddlers, this is usually between ages 1 and 1 ½.

Unlike infant car seats, convertible car seats do not have a base, so they're a bit more cumbersome. If you have a small vehicle, look for a compact seat to save space but also give your little one some more room to stretch out.

How is Mom?

Most women find that they are finally feeling more like themselves by the one-year mark, but this isn't always the case. If your partner has lingering problems due to pregnancy and childbirth, encourage her to take time to see her care provider this month. Specifically, if she has incontinence or other pelvic floor issues, discomfort at her c-section incision site, pain during intercourse, or if she is struggling to get back to a healthy weight, she should seek assistance.

How is Dad?

You've made it through your first year as a new dad - you deserve to celebrate! Schedule a time this month to have a one-year birthday date with your partner and toast all the ups and downs this year has brought.

Tips for a Successful First Birthday Party

Last-Minute Preparations

You've probably already sent invitations and gotten started your birthday party preparations, but if not, here are some last-minute items to get ready for the big day:

- **Review the Guest List:** You've already sent the invitations, so make sure to sit down and review the guest list to make sure you've included everyone you want to invite. Reach out to anyone who hasn't RSVP'd yet to see if they will be there for the big day.

- **Plan the Menu:** If you're serving food at the birthday party, you'll need to decide whether you will make the food yourself or outsource. Personally, unless you *love* cooking, I recommend outsourcing. Stores like Sam's or Costco have affordable party trays that will feed a crowd on a reasonable budget - and their items are pretty tasty, too! And don't forget beverages. Plan to get plenty of bottled water, and make a list of other beverages you want to serve.

- **Choose a Theme:** Choosing a theme for a party isn't just fun - it's also a great way to simplify things. Common first birthday party themes could be something related to baby's favorite toy or character (for example, a Winnie the Pooh party or a woodland animal party are popular options). Or it could be more abstract, like a color/pattern theme or food item (for example, pink polka dots or a fruit theme). Or you could choose something seasonal, like autumn leaves or a summer beach theme.

- **Select the Cake:** Once you have the guest list, menu, and theme selected, it's time to figure out the main event: cake! If you plan to host a large party, a sheet cake or two is ideal. For smaller events, you could serve cupcakes or even cake pops. If a lot of your guests have food allergies, plan to have a second cake available that is safe for them to eat.

Tips for the Day of the Party

The big day has finally arrived! It's easy to get so wrapped up in the excitement - and yes, the stress - of your baby's party that you don't have the chance to enjoy yourself. Here are my top 3 tips for keeping party day fun for everyone:

1. Be Strategic With Timing: I always reassure new parents that they don't have to plan their life around the baby's sleep

schedule, but this day is an exception. Plan the party for the time of day when your baby is awake, happy, and hungry.

2. Get Help With Cleanup: Ask a few close family members or friends to pitch in with cleanup. Or if you have any responsible teenage nieces or nephews, offer them a small stipend in return for cleanup help. Not having to worry about cleanup will minimize stress and allow you to enjoy the party (and maybe even take a nap when it's over!).

3. Keep it Short and Simple: Of course you want to celebrate this event, but when it comes to birthday parties for kids this age, simplicity and brevity are key. Schedule the party for no more than a few hours, and keep the decorations simple and easy. You'll have plenty of time for more complicated party schemes when your little one is older and more able to appreciate the details!

Of course, you and your partner will want to celebrate as well. One of my favorite birthday parties we hosted was my son's second birthday party. We had a late afternoon party with four of our close friends who also had children of similar ages. After the party was over and the kids were tired out, we had a few trusted babysitters come to our house to take care of the kids for a few hours while the parents went to a baseball game, sans kiddos. The kids had a great time with each other, and it was pretty fun to celebrate the first year of parenting with our friends, too.

One other tip - if you expect a lot of your baby's similarly-aged friends to be at the party with their parents, be sure to have a changing station set up, as well as a quiet area where parents can take their little ones if they get overwhelmed. Not all babies are social butterflies, and they might need a break from the excitement.

Between checkups, birthday parties, and all the everyday busyness this age brings, the twelve-month mark is an exciting time. Congratulations on your baby's first year - it's a big parenting milestone for you and your partner, too.

CHAPTER 11

PARENTING STYLES 101

WHAT'S *YOUR* PARENTING STYLE?

IN RECENT YEARS, there's been a lot of talk about different parenting styles or philosophies. With the rise of social media, it's easier and easier for people to share their opinions on the "best" way to raise your kids (for better or worse).

I like to tell a story about one guy knew who was totally stressed about being a new dad. As he and I were talking about it one day, he mentioned something about EC. I asked him what that was and he told me it stood for "elimination communication," which is basically a way of potty training your newborn right from the get-go.

Yes, you heard me right - he was trying to potty-train his newborn. No wonder he was stressed out!

As we kept talking, it became clear that he and his partner had been duped. They truly believed that by not following this ideology and practicing EC, they were dooming their child to a life of depression, health problems, relationship issues, and all kinds of other problems.

But the question they weren't asking was: how is this affecting my relationship with my child and my partner *now*? Is it more important that my 2-week-old baby poops in the toilet or that we're all getting enough sleep? Is following this parenting style and sticking with EC interfering with my mental health and that of my partner?

Don't get me wrong - I have nothing against anyone who practices EC. If it works for you, that's awesome! But clearly, it wasn't working for my friend.

This is just an example of the danger of clinging to a parenting style and its tenets without asking what is best for you, your partner, and your baby. Don't fall into this trap!

Instead, think of the first year of your baby's life as a time of discovery. Rather than adopting one parenting style dogmatically, remember that your ideas will grow and develop over time - and there's nothing wrong with that!

With all that said, let's take a look at some of the popular parenting styles out there.

ATTACHMENT PARENTING

What It Is

Attachment parenting became widely popularized by pediatrician Dr. William Sears, whose book *The Baby Book* took the parenting world by storm. Attachment parenting is based on the idea that children need to connect with their parents early on in order to form a relationship of trust. This parenting style features the 5 B's:

1. Birth bonding
2. Breastfeeding
3. Baby wearing
4. Bed sharing
5. Being responsive

Today, attachment parenting is one of the most popular parenting styles, especially with new parents. I think a lot of this has to do with the wide body of literature Dr. Sears and other AP proponents have written about the first year of life. Whereas some parenting books are more appropriate for parenting older kids and teens, attachment parenting begins before the baby is even born.

Pros and Cons

Pros:

- Attachment parenting has been shown in studies to reduce stress in children and also help them regulate their emotions.
- There's lots of literature out there about attachment parenting, making it accessible and easy to learn about.
- Since attachment parenting focuses on following the baby's cues, it can result in less frustration - babies are fickle!
- Some parents find it less stressful to have the baby hang out with them all the time.

Cons:

- Following attachment parenting principles to a T is hard! Some parents may find baby wearing, bed sharing, and breastfeeding on demand to be impractical for their life situations.
- Attachment parenting doesn't give some parents enough space. You might feel overwhelmed if your baby is constantly with you.

AUTHORITATIVE/PARENT-LED PARENTING

What It Is

Authoritative parenting (not to be confused with "authoritarian parenting," which is very different) was first developed as a concept by clinical psychologist Diane Baumrind in the 1960s. Authoritative parenting was the style she favored and put forth as the best. This parenting style combines setting firm limits through positivity. Unlike authoritarian parenting, which is often called "drill sergeant" style parenting, authoritative parenting supports the idea that while children need to observe boundaries, they shouldn't be coerced into following rules.

It can be hard to see how to apply these ideas during infancy. After all, authoritative parenting is all about communication - and your baby can't talk! However, as I've noted in previous chapters, getting to know your baby starts now. If you are attracted to the basic idea behind authoritative (also known as parent-led) parenting, you can see these first few years as a good practice run in patient communication and trying to meet your baby's needs.

Pros and Cons

Pros:

- Some children who are raised in a parent-led environment tend to be less likely to rebel and make harmful choices later in life
- Other studies show that parent-led approaches result in greater empathy and conscientiousness later in life

Cons:

- Hard to apply these principles during infancy
- This parenting style requires that parents take time to have an open dialogue with their kids - and as wonderful as that sounds, it can be challenging!

FREE-RANGE PARENTING

What It Is

Free-range parenting became all the rage in many parenting circles after the release of Lenore Skenazy's book *Free Range Kids* in 2009. This excerpt from the book's introduction provides some insight as to the basic gist of what this parenting style is all about (it's actually a hilarious book - I recommend reading it!):

"Somehow, even those of us who looked forward to parenting without too much paranoia have become anxious about every possible weird, scary, awful thing that could ever, just maybe, God forbid!, happen to our kids - from death by toilet drowning to stranger abduction to electrical outlet cover ingestion. Yes, I just read that those little plastic things you stick in the outlets to prevent baby electrocution turn out to be potential choking hazards. Just *try* not to worry."

As the name of the book suggests, this style of parenting encourages parents to allow their children to be free from excessive amounts of scheduling, rules, and safety measures. It's a controversial style of parenting because sometimes it's hard to gauge how much independence is too much, and vice versa, but the overall emphasis on helping kids discover freedom and "just let kids be kids" is definitely popular. Not to mention, it's a bit refreshing to be able to take a step back as a parent and enjoy the simple act of watching your baby develop without worrying about whether he's on track or following all the rules.

It might seem like this parenting style is a better fit for parents of older children, but I find a lot of free-range parenting concepts to be helpful during infancy. For example, I remember when our oldest was a baby, I was hyper-vigilant about knowing when she was going to eat, sleep, meet new milestones, and everything else babies do. I would get frustrated when sleeping schedules that had been working for weeks would suddenly fall apart or when a routine we had been keeping up with suddenly became unsustainable.

I quickly realized so much of my baby's life is out of my control and difficult - if not impossible! - to plan in advance.

Free-range parenting wasn't a thing back then, but if it had been, maybe I would have been able to chill out a little bit more! The general impulse to allow children to grow and develop in the way that is best for them is my key takeaway from free-range parenting styles.

Pros and Cons

Pros:

- Encourages flexibility in parents as the baby goes through changes that are often unpredictable
- May reduce parental anxiety because it prepares you for the unpredictability of parenting

Cons:

- Some parents may need more structure than this parenting style advocates
- It's easy for free-range parenting to be misunderstood as permissive parenting, a.k.a., letting your child do whatever he or she wants, which can be neglectful on the parent's part.

GREEN OR ECO-FRIENDLY PARENTING

What It Is

Green parenting, also known as eco-friendly or earth-friendly parenting, is a relatively new parenting style that has really only been developed in the last few years. As climate change has become more of a hot-button issue, parents have taken note and sought out ways to make child-rearing as environmentally responsible as possible.

This might sound like overkill, but the reality is clear: a lot of single-use products that have been proven to contribute to environmental decline are related to parenting. Case in point: disposable diapers.

Green parenting advocates a decreased reliance on single-use products and emphasizes a DIY approach to child-rearing. Here are a few common green parenting practices:

- Cloth diapering
- Making baby food at home

- Exclusive breastfeeding for at least 6 months
- Extended breastfeeding (breastfeeding beyond 2 years)

There really isn't a founder of green parenting - instead, it has emerged as a bit of a grassroots effort. Green parenting groups (also called natural parenting or ecological parenting) are very common on social media channels.

Pros and Cons

Pros:

- Environmentally sustainable
- Some practices - such as making baby food at home - could minimize your baby's exposure to harmful ingredients

Cons:

- Many environmentally-friendly practices (such as cloth diapering or making homemade food) are much more difficult and time-consuming

These are only a few of the many parenting styles out there. It can be a little overwhelming to try to keep up with all these ideas and approaches, but the one thing you *can* work on now that never goes away is consistency. Study after study shows that parents who are consistent in their approach are successful in the long run. Just like a dependable routine helps your baby feel secure and loved, consistency in your approach to parenting will provide a nurturing space for your child to grow and thrive.

But at the same time, keep in mind that your baby is still very young! It's not the case that you have to choose one of these parenting styles and stick to it for the rest of your life. I like to think of them as springboards. All these styles offer some good ideas (and maybe some not-so-good ideas) for you and your partner to ponder together. Your style ten years from now may be very different from the way it looks now. The most important factor is that you remain in open communication and work together to develop your parenting style.

CHAPTER 12
TAKING CARE OF YOUR RELATIONSHIPS

YOU'VE HEARD THIS BEFORE, but that's because it's true: the first step to solving any problem is admitting it exists. If you and your partner have taken that step, you are already on the way to improving your relationship.

If you haven't experienced relationship issues since your baby's birth, you're fortunate. Relationship issues are incredibly common in the first year postpartum. Couples who went through a traumatic birth experience are even more prone to difficulties, according to recent research in *Frontiers in Psychology Journal.* And if you or your partner suffers from postpartum depression, you are also at a higher risk of relationship problems.

Once you and your partner have agreed you want to work on your relationship, it can be difficult to know where to begin. I highly recommend couples therapy as a starting point. A counselor can evaluate you and your partner for signs of postpartum depression and provide treatment options, including talk therapy or medication. Even if you or your partner aren't diagnosed with postpartum depression, couples therapy is a great way to connect on a regular basis with an unbiased therapist who can help you sort through the challenges of new parenthood.

Aside from couples therapy, it's important to prioritize regular time together. Set aside time at least once a week to just be together or do something you enjoy as a couple.

SELF-CARE AND WHERE TO FIND SUPPORT

In addition to spending quality time with your partner, there are two other aspects of nurturing your relationship that many people overlook. First is the need for **self-care**. That's exactly what it sounds like: taking care of yourself. Here are a few self-care practices I recommend for new dads:

1. **Meditation**: I know, I know - that sounds weird. But meditation has become increasingly popular due to its amazing effects on mental health and well-being. There are a lot of apps that teach simple meditation practices. One of my favorites is Healthy Minds, which combines simple meditations with short podcast-style lectures about the benefits of meditation. Taking just five minutes per day made a huge difference in my patience, anxiety levels, and stress levels.
2. **Exercise:** Exercise is a must for anyone who wants to practice self-care and improve their mood, not to mention their physical fitness. Take time at least once a week to play a sport you like or do a type of exercise you enjoy. The enjoyment factor is crucial here because you'll be much more likely to follow through if you choose a physical activity you look forward to.
3. **Sleep:** Getting enough sleep at night might seem like an impossible dream during your baby's first year, but if you're experiencing trouble in your relationship or mood challenges, it's critical you find a solution. Consider hiring a postpartum doula to help for a few weeks so you can get some good shut-eye, or schedule a daily rest time after work to help you unwind and relax. Avoid caffeine after 3 pm, and talk to your doctor if you start to experience symptoms of insomnia, like

premature waking, sleeplessness, extreme tiredness during the day, or problems with memory and focus.

Aside from self-care, the second aspect of nurturing your relationship is **reaching out for support.** As studies have revealed more about the prevalence of postpartum relationship challenges, couples' support groups have become increasingly popular. Support groups meet to discuss common challenges new parents face or to share experiences with postpartum mood disorders. It's easy to feel isolated and alone when you're having relationship struggles, so it can be a huge relief to talk to other parents who are in the same boat. To find couples' support groups in your area, talk to your doctor or counselor and ask for recommendations.

FINANCES

Finances are a leading cause of strife in any relationship. When you factor in all the costs associated with having a baby, it's not surprising that money might cause a rift in your relationship.

In addition to discussing financial issues with your counselor, it's important to recognize that we all have different money personalities. Your partner might be your polar opposite when it comes to how she handles her money - but that doesn't have to mean imminent disaster. Like any other relationship issue, the key is to take the time to understand each other so you can work together and not be at odds.

Here are the seven most common money personalities, according to Ken Honda, author of the book *Happy Money* (which I highly recommend):

- Compulsive Saver: Saves money obsessively, is afraid of unnecessary spending
- Compulsive Spender: Spends money as an emotional response, feels remorse

- Compulsive Money-Maker: Prioritizes high income and craves recognition for wealth
- Indifferent-to-Money: Doesn't really care about money but is often in a good financial position
- Saver-Splurger: Combination of Saver and Spender
- Gambler: Combination of Spender and Moneymaker, takes large risks with money
- Worrier: Always worried about money and afraid of lack of freedom

Taking the time to identify which personality you and your partner have will go a long way in helping you achieve financial balance.

And of course, knowing what to expect in your child's first year of life also helps alleviate some of the stress you might feel about finances. For example, childcare can be very costly, so be sure to sit down several months before you start sending your baby to daycare and budget carefully for the costs.

New Dad Tips and Tricks

When our first child was born, I have to admit I was a little clueless about some of the challenges the first year would bring for my relationship with my partner. After an unexpected cesarean section, a challenging recovery, and a two-week stay in the hospital due to a severe breast infection that turned into abscesses, it's safe to say she and I were both a little stressed.

Now, six kids later, I can look back and see there were things I could have done differently that would have helped minimize the stress. Do I feel guilty I didn't do them then? No. As they say, hindsight is 20/20. But I would be remiss if I didn't share some of the lessons I've learned throughout my years as a dad. So without further ado, to conclude this chapter I thought I would include my top 3 new dad tips and tricks to relationship success.

1. **Anticipate Her Needs.** Don't wait for your partner to ask you to do some dishes or pick up the baby when he's crying. Just do it. A lot of times, we new dads feel a little reticent to offer help. Why? A lot of reasons. You might doubt your ability, or maybe you think your partner would rather just do the task herself. In my experience, the best strategy is to ask yourself, "What would I *really* want to be done right now if I were in her shoes?" If the sink full of dishes is calling out to you, don't even ask if she wants you to wash them. I can guarantee she won't complain if you take action without checking in first.

2. **Prioritize Togetherness.** If you're experiencing relationship struggles, that's your priority. Work, chores, and social expectations can wait. Find something you enjoy doing together, and do it every day. That could be taking a walk around the block, playing a game, or watching your favorite show. Whatever it is, make it the priority of your day.

3. **Say "Thank You":** Your partner has gone through a lot this year, and the words "thank you" are always welcome. Practicing gratitude has been shown to have huge benefits for mental health, and it's a great way to improve your relationship, as well. Compliment your partner often and tell her she's doing a good job.

Finally, don't forget physical affection. If your partner is struggling with intercourse, as is common in the first year postpartum, this can be sensitive, but remember - simple things like eye contact, a hug, or just holding hands can be great ways to show your love and gratitude.

Relationship struggles are common in the first year, but that doesn't mean they are inevitable. Being attentive to your partner's needs, prioritizing quality time, and displaying gratitude and affection will all help you weather the storm and get through your first twelve months as a family of three.

I'm sure the first year as a new dad has had its ups and downs - after all, you've done a pretty amazing and challenging thing this year. You have welcomed a new human being into your life, helped your partner recover from pregnancy and childbirth, and learned a lot about your own limits and potential. And if you're like me, you've probably also learned that fatherhood isn't just something that happens overnight - it's a constant journey.

This year you've watched your son or daughter develop from a tiny, helpless infant into a headstrong, mobile toddler. Through it all, your presence has made a huge difference. Fathers who are involved in their baby's life from the beginning not only feel closer to their children in the early years, but also set them up for success later in life. So keep up the great work - the adventure is just getting started!

Please leave a review.

If this book has helped you in any way, please leave a review so that others will find the book as well. Thank you for reading.

Click To Leave Review

Scan to leave a review.

RESOURCES

Attachment Parenting International. (n.d.).

https://www.attachmentparenting.org/

CDC (2022). *Immunization Schedules by Age.* AAP

https://www.cdc.gov/vaccines/schedules/downloads/child/0-18yrs-child-combined-schedule.pdf

Centers for Disease Control and Prevention. (n.d.) *Milestone Checklist.*

https://www.cdc.gov/ncbddd/actearly/pdf/FULL-LIST-CDC_LTSAE-Checklists2021_Eng_FNL2_508.pdf

Ernst, H. (2018) *Timeline of Postpartum Recovery.* Healthline.

https://www.healthline.com/health/postpartum-recovery-timeline

Griffin, R. (2021). *How Will My Premie Grow and Develop From Birth to Age 2?* WebMD.

https://www.webmd.com/parenting/baby/preemie-development-birth-age-2

FREE BONUSES

Free Bonus #1   Baby Financial Planning

In this book, you will learn all about the financial considerations of having a baby.

Free Bonus #2 10 Activities to Learn Parenting Skills

In this book, you will get tips on how to build parenting skills even before the baby is born.

Free Bonus #3 Authentic Connections

In this book, you will learn new skills to help you nurture your connection with your partner and bring it to a whole new level.

ABOUT THE AUTHOR

New Dad Support consists of dads and parenting professionals and experts whose passion is sharing their experience and expertise with new dads and dads-to-be.

BIBLIOGRAPHY

AAP (2022). *How to Keep Your Sleeping Baby Safe: AAP Policy Explained.* HealthyChildren.org. https://www.healthychildren.org/English/ages-stages/baby/sleep/Pages/A-Parents-Guide-to-Safe-Sleep.aspx

Alabama Public Health (n.d.). *Stomach Capacity https://www.alabamapublichealth.gov/perinatal/assets/ StomachCapacity.pdf*

Apgar Score. (2015). ACOG. https://www.acog.org/clinical/clinical-guidance/committee-opinion/articles/2015/10/the-apgar-score

Attachment Parenting International. (n.d.). https://www.attachmentparenting.org/

Babies stir up clouds of bio-gunk when they crawl. (n.d.). EurekAlert! https://www.eurekalert.org/news-releases/833043

Baby's First Tooth: 7 Facts Parents Should Know. (n.d.). HealthyChildren.org. https://www.healthychildren.org/English/ages-stages/baby/teething-tooth-care/Pages/Babys-First-Tooth-Facts-Parents-Should-Know.aspx

Bigelow, A. E. (2020). *Mother–Infant Skin-to-Skin Contact: Short- and Long-Term Effects for Mothers and Their Children Born Full-Term.* Frontiers. https://www.frontiersin.org/articles/10.3389/fpsyg.2020.01921/full

Brown, L. C. (2021, April 12). *Managing plugged ducts, mastitis when breastfeeding.* Mayo Clinic Health System. https://www.mayoclinichealthsystem.org/hometown-health/speaking-of-health/managing-plugged-ducts-mastitis-when-breastfeeding

Canadian Pediatric Society. (2012) *Preventing choking and suffocation in children.* Pediatrics and Child Health. https://academic.oup.com/pch/article/17/2/91/2638862

CDC (2022). *Immunization Schedules by Age.* AAP https://www.cdc.gov/vaccines/schedules/downloads/child/0-18yrs-child-combined-schedule.pdf

Cheng, C. (2018) *Supporting Fathering Through Infant Massage.* The Journal of Perinatal Education. https://connect.springerpub.com/content/sgrjpe/20/4/200.abstract

DeGroot, DW. (2021) *The effect of pregnancy and the duration of postpartum convalescence on the physical fitness of healthy women.* PLos One. https://www.ncbi.nlm.nih.gov/pmc/articles/PMC8318247/

Dewar, G. (2022, March 11). *The authoritative parenting style: An evidence-based guide.* PARENTING SCIENCE. https://parentingscience.com/authoritative-parenting-style/

The Effect of Kangaroo Care on Breastfeeding and Development in Preterm Neonates. (2021). Journal of Pediatric Nursing. https://www.sciencedirect.com/science/article/abs/pii/S0882596321000609#:~: text=Kangaroo%20care%20stabilizes%20the%20neonate's,and%20increases%20breast%20milk% 20intake.

Erlandsonn, K. (2007) *Skin-to-skin care with the father after cesarean birth...*Birth. https://pubmed.ncbi. nlm.nih.gov/17542814/

Explore how to tell if your baby is hungry. (2019, August 13). Comotomo. http://www.comotomo.com/ hungry-baby-feeding-cues-and-stomach-size/

Faure, M., & Richardson, A. (2012). *Baby Sense: Understanding your baby's sensory world - the key to a contented child* (1st ed.). Metz Press.

Fisher, D. (2018) *Fathers in neonatal units: Improving infant health by supporting the baby-father bond.* Journal of Neonatal Nursing. https://www.sciencedirect.com/science/article/abs/pii/ S1355184118300930

Food Allergy Nottingham (n.d.) *Are you sure it's lactose intolerance and not delayed cow's milk allergy?* https://www.foodallergynottingham.co.uk/news/are-you-sure-its-lactose-intolerance-and-not-delayed-cows-milk-allergy

Garthus-Niegel, S. (2018). *The Impact of Postpartum Posttraumatic Stress and Depression Symptoms on Couples' Relationship Satisfaction: A Population-Based Prospective Study.* Frontiers. https:// www.frontiersin.org/articles/10.3389/fpsyg.2018.01728/full

Goodman, J. (2003) *Paternal postpartum depression, its relationship to maternal postpartum depression, and implications for family health.* Journal of Advanced Nursing: https://onlinelibrary. wiley.com/doi/abs/10.1046/j.1365-2648.2003.02857.x

"Green" parenting tips. (n.d.). UNICEF. https://www.unicef.org/armenia/en/stories/green-parenting-tips

Harrington, C. T. (2022, June 1). *Butyrylcholinesterase is a potential biomarker for Sudden Infant Death Syndrome.* eBioMedicine. https://www.thelancet.com/journals/ebiom/article/PIIS2352-3964(22)00222-5/fulltext

Hewitt, L. (2020) *Tummy Time and Infant Health Outcomes: A Systematic Review.* Pediatrics. https:// publications.aap.org/pediatrics/article/145/6/e20192168/76940/Tummy-Time-and-Infant-Health-Outcomes-A-Systematic?autologincheck=redirected?nfToken=00000000-0000-0000-0000-000000000000

Hock, E. and Schirtzinger, M. (1992). *Maternal Separation Anxiety*. Society for Research in Child Development. https://srcd.onlinelibrary.wiley.com/doi/abs/10.1111/j.1467-8624.1992.tb03598.x

Honda, K. (2022, October 7). *There are 7 money personality types, says psychology expert. Which one are you?* CNBC. https://www.cnbc.com/2021/04/28/7-money-personality-types-and-the-pitfalls-of-each.html

Hui-Chin, H. (2004) *Antecedents and consequences of separation anxiety in first-time mothers*. Infant Behavior and Development. https://www.sciencedirect.com/science/article/abs/pii/S0163638304000141

Iftikhar, N., MD. (2020, June 30). *Dunstan Baby Language*. Healthline. https://www.healthline.com/health/baby/dunstan-baby-language

Information and Treatment for Postpartum Pelvic Floor Issues. (n.d.). Lifespan. https://www.lifespan.org/centers-services/pelvic-floor-disorders/conditions-we-treat/information-and-treatment-postpartum

Journal of Pediatrics (2014) *Infant Deaths and Injuries Associated With Wearable Blankets, Swaddle Wraps, and Swaddling* - NIH. (2014). https://pubmed.ncbi.nlm.nih.gov/24507866/

Karp, H. (2020) *The Happiest Baby Book – Fully Revised*. Happiest Baby. https://www.happiestbaby.com/products/the-happiest-baby-book-paperback

WIC (n.d.). *Low Milk Supply*. WIC Breastfeeding Support. https://wicbreastfeeding.fns.usda.gov/low-milk-supply

MacDonald, J. (2020) *How are you sleeping?* Journal of Affective Disorders. https://www.sciencedirect.com/science/article/abs/pii/S0165032720330111

Masters, M. (2022, August 23). *When Baby Growth Spurts Happen and the Signs to Look For*. What to Expect. https://www.whattoexpect.com/first-year/ask-heidi/baby-growth-spurts.aspx

Miller, P. (2014) *The benefits of attachment parenting for infants and children*. APA PsycNet. https://psycnet.apa.org/fulltext/2014-55579-001.html

Miller, R. *What Is the Experience of Babywearing a NICU Graduate?* Nursing for Women's Health. https://www.sciencedirect.com/science/article/abs/pii/S1751485120300726

NCBI. (2020). *Associations Between Mother-Infant Bed-Sharing Practices and Infant Affect and Behavior during the Still-Face Paradigm*. NIH. https://www.ncbi.nlm.nih.gov/pmc/articles/PMC7704549/

NCT. (2022, July 27). *Bleeding after birth: 10 things you need to know NCT*. NCT (National Childbirth Trust). https://www.nct.org.uk/life-parent/your-body-after-birth/bleeding-after-birth-10-things-you-need-know

Neuman, A. (2022, September 28). *How to Teach Baby 25 Key Words in Baby Sign Language*. https://www.thebump.com/a/how-to-teach-baby-sign-language

NHS website. (2021, November 18). *What should I do if I think my baby is allergic or intolerant to cows' milk?* nhs.uk. https://www.nhs.uk/common-health-questions/childrens-health/what-should-i-do-if-i-think-my-baby-is-allergic-or-intolerant-to-cows-milk/

Pecora, G. (2022, May). *Infant sleep and development*. Infant Behavior and Development. https://www.sciencedirect.com/science/article/abs/pii/S0163638322000339

Perkin, M. R., PhD. (2018, August 6). *Association of Early Introduction of Solids With Infant Sleep: A Secondary Analysis of a Randomized Clinical*. https://jamanetwork.com/journals/jamapediatrics/article-abstract/2686726

Premies: Breastfeeding. (2020, August 6). La Leche League International. https://www.llli.org/breastfeeding-info/premies-breastfeeding/

Quillin, S. (2004). *Interaction Between Feeding Method and Co-Sleeping on Maternal-Newborn Sleep*. Journal of Obstetric, Gynecologic, and Neonatal Nursing. https://pubmed.ncbi.nlm.nih.gov/15495703/

Ri-Hua, X (2009) *Prenatal Social Support, Postnatal Social Support, and Postpartum Depression*. Annals of Epidemiology. https://www.sciencedirect.com/science/article/abs/pii/S1047279709000799

Scarff, J. (2019) *Postpartum Depression in Men*. Innovations in Clinical Neuroscience. https://www.ncbi.nlm.nih.gov/pmc/articles/PMC6659987/

Sears, R (2022). *The Family Bed*. Parenting. https://www.parenting.com/baby/sleep/the-family-bed/

Scaccia, A. (2018, December 21). *Your Guide to Baby Massage*. Healthline. https://www.healthline.com/health/parenting/baby-massage

Skenazy, L. (2021). *Free-Range Kids: How Parents and Teachers Can Let Go and Let Grow*. Wiley.

Sleep Safety. (2022, November 14). Riley Children's Health. https://www.rileychildrens.org/health-info/sleep-safety

Unicef UK. (2022, February 13). *Co-sleeping guide for health professionals*. The Baby Friendly Initiative. https://www.unicef.org.uk/babyfriendly/baby-friendly-resources/sleep-and-night-time-resources/co-sleeping-and-sids/

Weisleder, A. and Fernald, A. (2013) *Talking to Children Matters: Early Language Experience Strengthens Processing and Builds Vocabulary.* Association for Psychological Science. https://journals.sagepub.com/doi/abs/10.1177/0956797613488145

Wen-Wang, R. (2020) *Prevalence of Prenatal and postpartum depression in fathers.* Journal of Affective Disorders. https://www.sciencedirect.com/science/article/abs/pii/S016503271931496X?via%3Dihub

Where We Stand: Vitamin D & Iron Supplements for Babies. (2022). HealthyChildren.org. https://www.healthychildren.org/English/ages-stages/baby/feeding-nutrition/Pages/Vitamin-Iron-Supplements.aspx

Zhao, T. and Kuhl, P (2016) *Musical intervention enhances infants' neural processing of temporal structure in music and speech.* PNAS. https://www.pnas.org/doi/pdf/10.1073/pnas.1603984113

Made in the USA
Columbia, SC
09 May 2023